Letters from a Shoebox

The Civil War Correspondence of John Huffman, David Huffman and William Bowman

JIM DOHREN

Letters from a Shoebox

For information about special discounts for bulk purchases, please contact Sunbury Press, Inc. Wholesale Dept. at (855) 338-8359 or orders@sunburypress.com.

To request one of our authors for speaking engagements or book signings, please contact Sunbury Press, Inc. Publicity Dept. at publicity@sunburypress.com.

FIRST SUNBURY PRESS EDITION
Printed in the United States of America
September 2013

Trade paperback ISBN: 978-1-62006-294-4
Mobipocket format (Kindle) ISBN: 978-1-62006-295-1
ePub format (Nook) ISBN: 978-1-62006-296-8

Published by:
Sunbury Press
Mechanicsburg, PA
www.sunburypress.com

Mechanicsburg, Pennsylvania USA

DEDICATION

When we read these letters we look back over a century and a half in wonder and admiration at the devotion and naiveté of the writers. While we can shake our heads at their gullibility, their honor and dignity deserve our respect.

These letters represent both a testament to trust and a responsibility to a legacy. Anne Huffman Bowman had faith that the letters that she cherished were important, and that they should be preserved for others who would understand their value. Thus, they came to Hugh, Lillian and Jerry Daugherty who maintained the trust. That responsibility was passed on to me.

I have invested so much in these letters and have such high regard for the love, faithfulness, courage, and sacrifice of their writers, that I have been guarded about sharing them. Now I submit them to you, trusting that you will honor and respect them for what they divulge and share the affection that I have for those who wrote them.

I also want to mention my wife Susan, and daughters Jen and Sarah, for their support over the many years this project has developed.

I am grateful to Mary Nourie, my sister-in-law, a successful children's author for her guidance and encouragement.

FOREWORD

It's often said that no good deed goes unpunished, but of course it's untrue. That regrettable bit of cynicism may be a way of protecting ourselves from being caught doing something nice for somebody else. We Americans can be a cynical lot. We like to believe we're tougher and less sentimental than we really are. Or, maybe we're afraid of bragging or tempting fate. The prevailing attitude causes us to deflect any credit or payback when we do something unselfish for others. Despite this, we keep on doing good and being nice even without expectation of reward.

Sometimes our good intentions do reap a reward, but we don't initially recognize it. Such was the case with these old letters. They each tell their own story. However, how I came to have them is a nice story of its own. For what it's worth, here it is.

In 1984, Treva Dohren, my Mom, told me she and Dad, her beloved Les, were going to take a trip to southeast Ohio from their home in northern Illinois for what might prove to be Mom's last chance to visit with her remaining cousins and childhood friends. As a young boy, I'd been taken on one or two similar excursions and had strong, if limited, memories of them. Now, Dad was nearly 70 and in the early stages of Parkinson's disease, and Mom was not much of driver. The trip took place in the summer, so neither my daughters nor I were involved with school. What would it hurt, I thought, if my wife Sue, and daughters Jennie and Sarah, went along? I could relieve Dad of the driving chores and Mom of the worries about Dad driving. All of us would get a little "Roots" trip to a place and a life altogether different from the city life that the five of us (Dad included) had grown up knowing. I won't deny that one of the incentives for going was that Dad and Mom were paying all the expenses, an important consideration for a family living on a teacher's salary. So, I signed us up.

One thing I hadn't thought out too clearly was how six people, including four women (one of whom was my notoriously over-packing mother) and their luggage, were all going to fit into my folks' 1980 Cutlass. The answer was - very tightly. At least the Olds had air conditioning.

Sue and the girls did love to eat out and stay in motels, so that was a mitigating factor. It did go a way, I suppose, in making up for touring hamlets like Sherrodsville and Bergholz, and even bigger places like New Philadelphia, with all the driving, the getting in and out of the car, and the meeting of people. Sue and the girls were wonderful at being polite and keeping up a conversation. For me, it was a remembrance of those visits I'd made before and the beloved stories Mom told me about her childhood when I was a child myself. For the girls, Mom and Dad worked in a day at Sea World in Aurora, Ohio. Thoroughly enjoyed by all, it became the girls' favorite part of the trip.

For a week, we meandered through the hills of rural Ohio and absorbed or endured, as the case may be, the memories of a plain rural childhood. Eventually, we visited with Mom's delightful cousin, Hugh Daugherty, and his gracious wife, Lillian. We arrived at their home in Euclid, Ohio, in time for supper.

After supper, we went to the recreation room in the basement. Lillian mentioned that since I was a history teacher, she had something that she thought I might like to read. Being polite, I agreed. She went into a closet and came out with a shoe box. Inside was, and I kid you not, a hot dog bun wrapper enclosing packets wrapped in paper towels. Without any particular anticipation, I began to explore the contents.

Two things immediately became apparent. First, I had at my disposal a batch of original American Civil War letters; and second, I was going to become a very rude guest as I totally ignored all else going on around me. Though most of the letters were well-preserved, I could only read parts of them at the time due to aging coupled with vagaries of handwriting, spelling, and punctuation. Somehow, the end of the evening and the end of the letters coincided (or so I hope). Certainly, I expressed amazement and gratitude.

The next day we returned to Hugh and Lillian's for a cook-out with members of their family. We had a great time. As we were leaving, Lillian presented me with the shoe box of letters and asked if I'd like to keep them. I remember being stunned, not knowing what to say other than that they should stay in their family. She countered by saying that she and Hugh had talked it over and decided that no one in their family had shown as much interest or appreciation for them as I had. They felt that as an American history teacher, I might be able to use them to help my students. In one of my more enlightened moments, I agreed and took over responsibility for the collection.

Not long after I got home, I began to work on the letters. First, I made a hand-written draft of each letter. This was very time consuming, tedious work, but I didn't mind. In fact, I found it to be a deeply satisfying intellectual task. Over time, I became immersed in the writing and found myself speculating about the young men and women who wrote them.

Next, I made a second transcription, typing the letters into an Apple IIe computer, and saving them on diskettes. As I transcribed and learned more information, I began to do some research. I sent to the Bureau of Archives and found much information. Ironically, among other things, I learned that I could find out a lot more about the records of Civil War soldiers than I could about my uncle's WWII records due to a devastating fire at the St. Louis documents center. On a school trip to Washington, D.C., I took a couple of free hours and stopped by the Archives building to request some records in person.

As my research accumulated, I began adding supplemental material. I believed the letters deserved more than just a literal transcription. Then, too, I realized that not everyone who read them would have as much background information as I had. For that reason, I began to add the "Notes and Comments" section, a combination of research and personal thought.

I found that my cousin, Jerry Daugherty, whom I'd met at Hugh and Lillian's, had a few letters from the same family. We exchanged letters and information so that both of our collections became more complete.

I made a copy of all my work and sent it to Hugh and Lillian, along with my thoughts of gratitude for entrusting me with the letters. They returned a note letting me know how much they appreciated what I'd done with the collection.

All of this occurred prior to 1986. Then, except for a few public programs I gave centering on the letters, I pretty much let them alone. In 2009, lacking a focus for any other writing projects, I began to make an updated edition of the letters and my notes and comments. Not having any means to transfer or even print the files from the old Apple diskettes, I began from scratch. I used the copies I'd scanned of the originals, going back a few times to the safe deposit box to remove one of the originals for examination. I used my printed transcriptions and some additional information which had come to me over nearly 15 years. I was surprised by how much editing there was to do, but was pleased at how much better the new transcripts stayed true to the originals. I also created some additional documents: a chronological listing of letters, a listing and description of the correspondents, a historical perspective, an epilogue, and this foreword.

Then, as now, I marveled at the bravery which enabled men to engage in battle knowing full well that the odds of being maimed or killed were terribly high. Of course, I speculated on how I would fare as one of them. The letters from home added a dimension which was new, and nearly as captivating as the battlefield letters.

Before proceeding any further, I hasten to proclaim to all readers that I am not a Civil War scholar. I compiled all the writings that follow simply because I became increasingly fascinated as my imagination carried me farther and farther into thoughts about the letter writers. They renewed a fascination of 50 years ago when the centennial of Ft. Sumter prompted me to read the works of McKinley Kantor, Carl Sandberg, Bruce Catton, and others.

Some, perhaps many, who read the Notes and Comments in particular, will have just cause to question or doubt my interpretations. I do not dispute them. Be that as it may, I hope all who read the Shoebox Letters will find some affinity with those heroic folks who lived so long ago.

Jim Dohren 2013

JIM DOHREN

HISTORICAL PERSPECTIVE ON THE UNION CIVIL WAR POSTAL SYSTEM

Despite all its vacillations, negligence, massive waste and other blunders in determining a winning strategy the Federal forces did quickly and firmly grasp the concept that an efficient and cooperative postal system operating between servicemen and the home front was essential for good morale for troops who were all too often given good cause for being demoralized and morose. In an all too rare instance of military intelligence and common sense, the Federal government simply connected its field operations to the already existing postal service in the North.

Letters to the home front could take full advantage of the system. Letters to the field, however, were much more subject to arbitrary factors. Military cargoes and personnel were given priority over civilian passengers and mail, of course. Civilian postal problems were the same problems to which the military was prone, namely missing bridges, roads clogged with men, wagons, guns, horses and the seemingly omnipresent mud or its evil brother choking dust. Beyond that would be the confusion about where a regiment or company might even remotely be located since, for without understatement, it was not in the best interests of the military to make it easy for civilians to know this information.

Nonetheless, the military did make it a priority to keep the mail going. To that purpose every unit down to company had clerks assigned to collect the soldiers' letters and distribute letters from home. Mobile post offices were made available in wagons or tents in the field or crude frame structures built where there more permanent quarters. A soldier only had to write the words "soldier's letter" on the front of the envelope and the letter would be sent C.O.D. (collect on delivery). Back home the soldiers' letters found their way to rural post offices that might be found in a village building or private home where the home folks were glad to pay a penny or two for delivery.

While WWII letters home were notorious for being snipped to pieces by often over cautious censors looking for sensitive information the GI might have innocently given away, it was quite different during the Civil War. Unless there was the chance that military mail would pass across compromised territory (In this case think of the Army of The Cumberland and its March-to-the-Sea) soldier's letters weren't read, let alone censored. Unlike WWII where the speed of V-mail and air-mail made troop locations a vital secret, in the Civil War geographic or unit strength information would often be rendered irrelevant by the between the writing of a letter and its delivery.

Giving unit location and strength in their letters was one of the least considerations of the masses of ordinary soldiers. Their grasp of "The Big Picture" was illusive at best and besides, unless something big happened such as the Fall of Atlanta they were much more concerned with the overwhelming moral and physical fears and struggles of military life, concerned about the folks back home and starved for the knowledge that their family and friends were continuing to write.

Regarding the Shoebox Letters

Spelling variations have been left as I found them in the letters. The more that I became attuned to them, the less I wanted to be a critic. I felt that critical marks might be more distracting than helpful, and in a way, even disrespectful to the letter writers. I hope that readers will understand my reticence, and through more careful readings, particularly of William Bowman's letters, come to know the boys as I have.

Jim Dohren

LIST OF CORRESPONDENTS

William "Bill" Bowman (pronounced "Baughman") - William was a New Cumberland, Tuscarawas County, Ohio, farm hand boarding on the Daniel Huffman farm when he enlisted in the 126th Ohio Volunteer Regiment in 1862 for a period of three years. On his enlistment record, his age is listed as 19. However, his tombstone lists his birth year as 1845 which would make him 17 years old at the time of enlistment. His rank was private throughout his service. He was an infantryman.

John J. Huffman - John was a 29-year-old school teacher when he enlisted for three years in the early fall of 1862. Although his enlistment record indicates that he lived in New Cumberland, Ohio, he actually lived in Clay County, Indiana. He enlisted and served as a private in Company I of the 85th Indiana Volunteer Infantry. John's letters showed that he was a member of the ambulance corps and probably a hospital nurse, though he may also have been an infantryman for a time.

David L. Huffman - David was a 25-year-old school teacher when he enlisted in the late summer of 1862 for three years. He boarded on a farm in Indiana with his brother John. Both spent most of their lives in New Cumberland, Ohio. He enlisted and eventually served as a "2nd" Sergeant in Company I of the 85th Indiana Volunteer Infantry. He was in the ambulance corps like his brother and may have served in the regular infantry as well.

Matilda Huffman - Matilda was the wife of George Huffman, who was the older brother of John, David, Anne, and C.J., and thus was their sister-in-law. She lived in New Cumberland, Ohio. She was 24 years old in 1862.

C.J. Huffman - C.J., also known as Christiana, was a younger sister of Anne, John, David, and George, and the sister-in-law of Matilda. She was unmarried and lived in New Cumberland, Ohio, with her parents, Levi and Mary Huffman. She was 18 years old in 1862.

Eve Ann(e) Huffman – Anne did not write any of the letters in this collection. Most of the letters were written to her in response to letters she had written to her family, so she can be accurately described as a co-respondent. She was another younger sister of the Huffman brothers. She was living with a family in Indiana, probably in Middletown, in Henry County. None of the letters give a direct explanation for her residing away from New Cumberland. Anne is additionally a vital character in the correspondence for she is not only the object of it, but the one who originally prized the letters enough to keep them together and safe. She eventually moved back to Tuscarawas County, Ohio, and married William Bowman. She and William are my great, great aunt and uncle. Anne was 23 years old in 1862.

Ruth Davy - Ruth was a childhood friend and neighbor of Anne Huffman. She was 16 years old in 1862.

CHRONOLOGICAL LISTING OF THE LETTERS

1. Parkersburg, Virginia - William Bowman to David Huffman - early Civil War, late 1862

2. Parkersburg, Virginia - William Bowman to David Huffman - September 24, 1862

3. Martinsburg, Virginia - William Bowman to David Huffman - January 28, 1863

4. Danville, Kentucky - John Huffman to George Huffman (assumed) - February 13, 1863

5. Tullahoma, Tennessee - John Huffman to Anne Huffman - April 25, 1863

6. Possibly Chickamauga – exact location not stated – probably written by John Huffman - September 20-21, 1863

7. Fosterville, Tennessee - David Huffman to Anne Huffman - November 20, 1863

8. Kingston, Georgia - John Huffman to Anne Huffman - May 22, 1864

9. Camp Sumter, Georgia - William Bowman to David Huffman - June 2, 1864

10. New Cumberland, Ohio - Ruth Davy to Anne Huffman - June 6, 1864

11. New Cumberland, Ohio - Matilda Huffman to Anne Huffman - July 14, 1864

12. Atlanta, Georgia - John Huffman to Anne Huffman - September 11, 1864

13. New Cumberland, Ohio - Matilda Huffman to Anne Huffman - Sept. 28, 1864

14. Atlanta, Georgia - John Huffman to Anne Huffman - November 1, 1864

15. New Cumberland, Ohio - C.J. Huffman to Anne Huffman – November 3, 1864

16. New Cumberland, Ohio - Matilda Huffman to Anne Huffman- March 6, 1865

17. New Cumberland, Ohio - C.J. Huffman to Anne Huffman - March 9, 1865

18. Goldsboro, North Carolina - John Huffman to Anne Huffman - March 28, 1865

19. New Cumberland, Ohio - William Bowman to Anne Huffman - April 27, 1865

20. Raleigh, North Carolina - John Huffman to Anne Huffman - April 29, 1865

21. New Cumberland, Ohio - Matilda Huffman to Anne Huffman - May 18, 1865

22. Indianapolis, Indiana - John Huffman to Anne Huffman – June 28, 1865

1.
Parkersburg, Virginia
William Bowman to David Huffman
Early Civil War, late 1862

Tell John Mansfield that he should stay with Jim till I come home I think by the grace of God I will get home safe but if I do not get home to see you I hope to meat you in heaven There is a good deal of bad conduct here but Wes (probably Wes Hoopingarner) and I do not take any part in it and I thank god for it that he will protect us from any harm. I think he wil help us from being hurt we have to be very strict here what we drink for there was a man poisand here last night on whiskey but Wesley and I do not drink of the filthy stuf for tell the folks that I like it verry well here tell the boy that I would like to see them tell them that I will come home next spring the war will be at home tell our girls to be contented for I will see them again and and (written twice)
I must bring my letter to a close this lett is not wrote very plain let some of the boys read it if you can not. write soon as you get this letter and tell me how are a getting along I heard that you was a coming to Camp Steubenville to see me but was to late for we went away that day that Davy was here I wish that you had come with them to see us but you was to late we are about three hundred miles from home we came about five hundred miles to get here the river is to low to come on it we rode it on the cars write as soon as you get this letter direct to Camp Parkersburgh Woods County Virginia in care of Captain Oliver Franc 126 Regiment

William Bowman
David Huffman

The transcription of the letter was provided to me by Jerry Daugherty, my cousin. Jerry's parents provided me with the letters that I have. I have not seen a copy of the

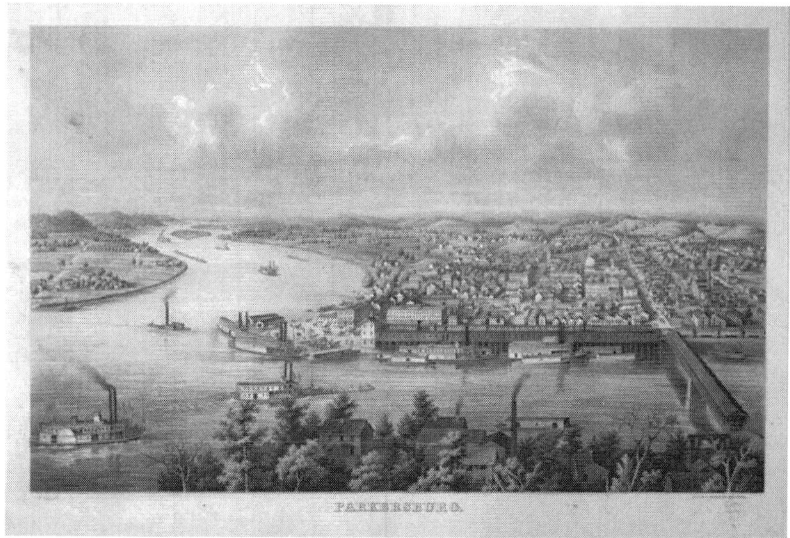

Parkersburg, Virginia (now West Virginia) circa 1861

original of this letter, so I have not had a chance to do my own transcription. Jerry has his own collection of letters – not as many from the Civil War soldiers, but many from the Huffman family members. These family letters add a lot of background to the story. The placing of this letter as "early Civil War, late 1862" is Jerry's. Evidently it wasn't dated by William, and Jerry didn't say why he dated it when he did.

Jerry states, "This letter is written on four 5"x5" pages of sturdy not paper stock, somewhat yellowed on page 1 and folded for a 3"x51/4" envelope. Pencil, sturdy writing, which is easily read except for the fading on the first page. Large "flourishy" scroll surrounding the final two names at the bottom of the last page. (Similar to other Parkersburg letter.)"

"Interesting comments on the characteristics of the people in Camp and almost raises some doubts as to whether he DOES protect himself from the evils of the Camp, by his strong protestations! I later got the impression that he truly was as 'Heaven-motivated' as he professes."

This is quite an affecting letter for its idealism, optimism, and faith. It's safe to call it naïve, I suppose, for those reasons. Certainly it's not in the same voice as letters we'll find William writing in 1864 and 1865. In 1862, we still hear the wonderment of a farm boy, maybe only a 16-year old farm boy at that, in an environment he is just getting used to. He is apologetic about his lack of writing skill and even suggests that David get someone else to read it to him. His homesickness and loneliness are apparent. Twice he digresses to talk either about camp life or how far he is from home. In particular, he mentions how the 126th got to Parkersburg ("We rode the cars", i.e. the railroad, perhaps an adventure in itself.) There is no mistaking that this letter is an appeal for news from home. Visits were no longer reasonable to expect, leaving letters as the sole means of maintaining a connection. The phrase "next spring the war will be at home" caught my eye. I haven't figured this out. Is it Jerry's misreading of the letter, or is William just writing his thoughts awkwardly? Without a copy of the original, I can't tell. But, here is what I think. Consider this confusing phrase in the following light. First, there is a longer than normal space after the words "next spring". If William was interrupted in his writing for any of a hundred reasons and came back to his letter to finish it in haste, he may well have lost his train of thought and conflated two related thoughts - "next year the war will be done" and "next Spring I will be at home. If so, this makes sense. He writes "and and", then in the next sentence writes that he must bring the letter to a close. William could well have assumed, as did the great majority of the citizens both North and South, that the war could not last longer than Spring, and that he would be home by then.

I have a theory for trying to establish which Parkersburg letter is earlier – this one or the one that follows. An interesting clue is posed by the sentence "I heard you was a coming to Camp Steubenville to see me but was too late for we went away that day that Davy was here". "Davy" certainly can't refer to David Huffman since the letter is written <u>to</u> him. Ohio's Civil War Regimental History shows that the 126th Ohio was organized at Camp Steubenville. The records do not specify when the process began, only that it was mustered in on Sept. 4, 1862 and sent to Parkersburg on the 16th. In addition, records confirm that no new regiments were formed anywhere near Rose Township or Tuscarawas or Carroll Counties for the remainder of the war. According to the 1860 Census, David and John Huffman were employed as school teachers in Indiana. The Huffmans' enlistment records show the two were enrolled in early August of 1862 and mustered in less than a month later in early September. In 1862, a journey from rural Ohio obviously took a significant amount of time.

My theory also answers the question of why the Huffman brothers didn't enlist in the 126th Ohio with William and others from the area. If the 126th was organized at Camp Steubenville in the late winter and early spring of 1862, and in training during the summer, the brothers would have been bound by teaching contracts which they honored. When the school term ended in April, it would have been too late to catch up with the 126th Ohio. In his letter, William may be referring to a possible visit that the brothers made home to New Cumberland, Ohio, earlier in the summer. He seems to be wishing that his friend David had come to Camp Steubenville while the regiment was still training. Obviously, the visit didn't happen. Since there were no new regiments organizing in Rose Township or Tuscarawas or Carroll Counties in Ohio, the Huffmans did the next best thing by going back to Indiana to enlist in the 85th IVI (Indiana Volunteer Infantry) where they would have had friends. Without the envelope and its intended address, it is difficult to know where William believes David is. If David (and perhaps John as well) had not yet left to enlist in Indiana and were still close enough to travel to Camp Steubenville, then this letter is probably the earlier of the two Parkersburg letters. If this is true, it would make this letter the earliest in the collection, having been written in late summer of 1862. Whatever the reason, enlisting in the 85th Indiana meant the Huffmans and William Bowman would never serve close to each other during the war. William would be in the Army of The Potomac, David and John in the Army of The Cumberland.

Another of the mysteries of this letter is the identity of the Davy that William writes about. Is this a first name or last? Actually, it's quite probable that it is a relative of

Ruth Davy who is another of the letter writers in the collection. In the 1860 census, the Davy family is listed as neighbors of the Huffmans. There is a father, E.D., and two older sons, Thomas, 20 years old, Abraham 18 years old, and Ruth who is 14. They would all be William's neighbors and friends. It's perfectly reasonable that one of them made the relatively short journey to Camp Steubenville to visit the New Cumberland boys.

Many of the letters in the collection are addressed to Anne Huffman. They indicate that she was living in Henry County, Indiana, during the war. It is difficult to know whether she was living there before, or relocated there because of her brothers. Census records aren't very precise. It's reasonable to speculate that the Huffmans may have had family or close friends living there, and she moved in with one of them. It's only a bit less speculative to consider that Anne may have gone to Indiana with her brothers and stayed there for some reason of her own. (Further in my research, I unearthed a clue as to her possible reason for moving there.)

After multiple readings of all William's letters, and considering his fate in the war, I have the same heartbreaking sense of fate when I reread this first letter of his. He instructs David to address future letters "in care of Captain Oliver Franc" (sic) the commanding officer of Company G. William twice mentions Wes (or Wesley). That would be Wes Hoopingarner, a neighbor of his in New Cumberland, and evidently a close friend who helps him resist evil. Captain France, William and Wesley serve through and survive many skirmishes and battles together until the Battle of The Wilderness. There, in the dying light of May 6, 1864, they, together with their comrades, endure the bloody chaos when the 126th Ohio is rolled up in a powerful flanking movement which comes without warning from the thick forest. Organization crumbles, and in the ensuing rout, Captain France is one of dozens killed or wounded. Both William and Wesley are lucky to be captured alive and at least physically unscathed. From there, the paths of the two friends soon diverge. In the 126th Ohio regimental muster rolls, Wesley is recorded as deserting on Aug. 12, 1864. This is before William is imprisoned at Camp Sumter, most likely after the pair spends time in Libby Prison. Wesley, however, doesn't merely desert. He takes an oath of allegiance to the Confederacy in exchange for papers of safe transit anywhere in the Confederate controlled territory. In one of his letters to Ann after his exchange, William has just cause when he scorns or perhaps mourns the weakness of his boyhood friend when he writes, "I will tell you a little about Wes Hoopingarner he deserted and joined the rebbel army I never thought he had that little principle a bout him as that come to he never need to came back to this country..." His words speak for themselves.

2.
Parkersburg, Virginia
William Bowman to David Huffman
September 24, 1862

Septtember the 24
(year is illegible but is probably 1862)

Mr. David Huffman Dear Sir I take my pen in hand to let you now that I am well at preasant and I hope that these few lines may find you in the same blessing of health
We are in par ker burgh in Virginia we expect an at tact here soon for there was on hundred fifty cavalry men come in here to day and if they do come in on us they will haft to have a greater force we can have ten thousand of men here in five hours we only have two thousand here now, but there is two thousand on the other side of the river that is a laing in the ambush watching for them to cross the Canawway (probably the Little Kanawha River) and they will fire [begin pg. 2] on them and we will come on them from this side (several words scribbled out here) We have ten pieces of cannon come in here to day it will make a hard fight but I do no believe it at all for there is to big a force here the president procolamation says that the war will be over in three months. If that is sow we will be home soon the war cannot last longer than spring. I think we will stay in parkers burgh all winter I have wrote you three or four letters and I have only got on I want you to write more to me for I want to now how you and the girls is a getting along and the nabours if they are well [end of pg. 2 and front of the letter]
I wrote John Mansfield one letter and tell him if he got my letter and till him to write to me as son as you get this letter and tell George Strawn to write to me for I would like to here from him and his family there is a greate deal of card playing a going on here but I have not touched a card since I have been in campe and I have not done any gambling here I dnot pay

anny attention to them. I read my testament verry near evry night for I go to bed I try to do right I want you serve the lord with all your hart and I will try to do the same [begin pg. 4] there is a great deal of wikedness in camp this is a hard place to do right but I have to put my trust in the lord and he gives me grace I always think he will save me from being killed I must bring my letter to a close write as soon as you get this letter direct to parkers burgh wood Virginia in car of Capt france

126 regiment
(There are three letters following which are hard to read but are logically "OVI" for Ohio Volunteer Infantry.)

(at the bottom set off with crude flourishes probably to clear the pen nib of wet ink):

William Bowman
to Mr. David Huffman
W.B.D.H.

Even though the last year of the date in this letter is unreadable, I am almost certain it was 1862. Corroboration for this is the fact that both letters were written from Parkersburg, Virginia. The 126th Ohio was not in Parkersburg from 1863-1865. Also, the other Parkersburg letter does have the full year listed as 1862. I am confident that the other letter is the first in the collection. William assumes that David Huffman is still at home in Tuscarawas County judging by his requests for local news and letters.

The cursive writing, spelling, grammar, and usage in this letter are much cruder than in either of the Huffman brothers' letters. It does make the letter more interesting, I suppose. Certainly, it made it much more of a challenge to interpret and transcribe. And it was more fun, too. It is worth noting that in his letter from New Cumberland dated April 27, 1865, William uses much better mechanics and penmanship. He also apologizes for his mistakes. I suspect the difference is that the 1865 letter was written to Miss Anne Huffman whom William eventually marries. He also may have had more time to write. He was home, and the war was over.

The handwriting begins fairly neatly, but deteriorates gradually until it is quite messy at the end as if the writer was running out of time or patience. William does mention having to bring the letter to a close, but that could be as much because he had run out of things to write or, equally, had run out of paper on which to write, as opposed to haste.

If William is a friend of David's to the point that he pairs their initials at the end of the letter, why does he twice address him as Mister David Huffman? Is this just politeness, or is there another reason? Does it show deference to David's older age or occupation as a school teacher? For that matter, could David and/or John have taught William? It may just be good humor between two young friends. I found the paired initials poignant for I think they show how much of a boy William still is.

Despite the rather crude handwriting and grammar, William is pretty formal in the way that he styles his letter. Letter writing was a most important form of communication in the 19th century, certainly one of the foremost reasons for learning to read and write. So it stands to reason that proper writing of a letter was a vital part of public instruction in rural as well as urban areas, perhaps more so due to the distances.

It is worth restating that William may have been quite young in 1862. Though his discharge form states that he was 22 years old in 1865, the dates on his tombstone shows a birth year of 1846. The difference could be accounted for by the fact that if the 1846 birth date is correct, he would have had to lie about his age to enlist in 1862. Perhaps he was advised to continue to overstate his age at discharge to avoid trouble. There were thousands of others who did the same. If that 1846 birth date is accurate, it would make him only 15 or 16 in 1862 when he wrote this letter. He was also a farm boy. Those two facts go a long way toward explaining his poor writing skills and his bewilderment over the "wikedness" of camp life. Hopefully, he would have been comforted by some of the many neighbors who would also have enlisted in the 126th Ohio. The 126th was a young and "green" outfit itself, having been mustered in only about three weeks earlier on Sept. 4, 1862. It didn't arrive in Parkersburg until September 16th.

This paper has no watermark or embossed maker's mark. It appears to be unlined, but the lines may have faded or a piece of dark-lined paper may have been put under it while William was writing. Despite the poor penmanship, the writing is straight, at least until page four.

3.
Martinsburg, Virginia
William Bowman to David Huffman
January 28, 1863

January the 28 AD 186[?] probably *<u>1863</u>*

Martinsburgh Virginia

Mr. David Huffman
Dear sir it is with pleasure that I seat mysealf this morning to let you now that I am well and I hope when thes few lines come to hand they find you the same greate blessing of health I have not received anny letter from you for a good while I would like to get word from you once more I tell you I am well satisfied in the army I have my health verry well since I left home there is a good many sick in this regiment [begin pg.2] there is seven died out of our regiment there was two died out of our company last weeke we discharge Jhon Albaugh last night he has got the palpitation of the heart I hope to god I will keep my health as well as I have I have mot much news to tell you Esra Albaugh is here to this morning he came after his son yesterday and he is a going to starte home with [him?] to day
[begin pg. 3] I do not want to get a discharge till the war is over if I keep my health I sent in my letter for you to send me some money in your next letter we have not anny money here we will get our money some time soon we will not get less than fifty or sixty dollars the next time and I will send you some I will make it all right when I get my money [begin pg. 4] if you send me some money I want to xxxxxx [illegible word due to being crossed out] have some money to have my boots half soled it takes one dollar for pair of half soles I would like for you to send some in your next letter write as soon as tis comes to hand

Direct to Martinsburgh Berkley Co virg

Company G 126 reg ovi in care of Cap't Gerome

William Bowman

David Huffman
tell John Mansfield to write to me

This is another of Jerry's letters. He notes: "Testy attitude, due to no letters, showing how important news from home was to them. They are fighting without benefit of pay for even the most important necessities. (It) emphasizes the Rag-tag (sic) condition of the forces".

I detected the same "testy" tone in this letter as Jerry did. It's hard to miss. Perhaps that is a more lenient way of analyzing William's attitude than to say that he is feeling a little sorry for himself when he writes this. If he's not

Rebel troops arriving and departing from Martinsburg, Virgina depicted in Harper's Weekly *June 29, 1861. Soon after Bowman's letter, West Virginia seceeded from Virginia and joined the Union.*

getting any news from home, no wonder there is further cause for a negative outlook.

As with John Huffman's first letter which comes next in the collection, this one gives stark testimony to support what we have read about the importance of good health and a strong constitution (what today we might call a healthy immune system) for Civil War soldiers. In one week, they have suffered two deaths from disease. If a company consists of about one hundred men, that is already a two percent casualty rate which doesn't even include those too sick to muster. In the regimental record of the men of the 126th Ohio, John Albaugh is indeed listed as being "discharged to date Jan. 23, 1863, on Surgeon's certificate of disability." In addition, James Casteel and Lemuel Barthalow were discharged for the same reason on January 3rd. John Domer, George Winter, Josiah Stevens, and David Resler are listed as having died of disease at Martinsburg. My research shows that the 126th was in Martinsburg to guard the Baltimore and Ohio Railroad. It remained there through the middle of June, when it was forced to retreat to Harper's Ferry under attack by Lee's forces.

As long as I am on the subject of casualties, I cannot ignore the high casualty rate of the 126th Ohio. I obtained a record that briefly lists William Bowman's war experiences along with that of thirty other soldiers. I found 18 casualties, five from illness (including two deaths), three captured, five wounded, and five killed in action. That adds up to a casualty rate approaching 60%! One man, Henry Devins, like William, was captured in the Wilderness Battle and interned at Andersonville. He died there on July 31, 1864.

The 126th was no ordinary regiment as it turned out. No one could have foreseen from its common enough beginning and early failure that it would become one of the most combat proven, reliable, and relied upon units in the Army of The Potomac. From duty to suppress the New York City draft riots to the Appomattox Campaign and beyond, the regiment earned a particularly auspicious reputation. William must have been very proud of this and his contributions to it.

William's letter also gives graphic support for our knowledge of the irregular pay of the troops. In the South, the problems were much worse as the currency was of little or no value. However, even the much wealthier Union had problems. The fifty or sixty dollars that William mentions may be several months' pay. This brought hardships for the men, even though they were still (hopefully) supplied with food by the government. The soldiers cooked and ate in small units as there were no large unit organized kitchens or "messes" as in later wars. Beyond the basics, the men had to pay for their own food. In addition, things which made life a little more comfortable or less boring had to be paid out of pocket. This included things like sewing and writing materials, books, cards, and liquor (not that William would spend any money on the latter two). William gives one example, but an important one, when he writes that he needs money to have his boots repaired. If they are worn out, then they will leak in wet weather and expose the soles of his feet to stones when marching. One dollar to half-sole a pair of boots seems high. In her letter to Ann(e), Matilda writes that her husband George was working for one dollar a day.

William asks three times for money in this letter. His first reference is to a previous request which has so far not been fulfilled by David. The other two simply show how desperate he is. He is anxious for David to know that he will pay him back as soon as possible.

Actually, it is interesting that William is still addressing letters to David even though David and John Huffman entered the service in Indiana nearly four months earlier. If he knows this, he certainly cannot hope David will have any money to send him from his own pay, or that David will even get his letter. Perhaps this apparent disconnect is because William is not receiving his letters. It also begs the question of how William's and John's letters to David came to be saved. How did Anne get them? One possibility is that they all indeed did reach David and were with his personal effects.

William makes neither further profession of religious faith, nor does he comment about the "wickedness" of camp and its temptations as he did in previous letters.

Does this show that he is becoming a seasoned soldier, accepting army life for what it is? Does it hint that he has succumbed to the temptations? Is his situation genuinely so extreme that his need for money lowers the priority of everything else? Or, can we conclude that William seems to be just what he is - a young farm boy far from home in a strange, threatening, and terrifying environment.

I have not seen this letter, so I cannot remark on the penmanship. However, the spelling, grammar, and other mechanics of this letter are consistent with others written by William. Jerry writes: "Written in brown ink on 8" x 10" paper double-folded to 5 x 8. (Note: The original ink color would not have been brown. The brown color is a result of the aging of chemicals in the ink used in old letters. Fortunately, it makes the letters more legible.) Very evenly spaced lines although no guide lines present, (as if written on paper placed over a master, ruled sheet like some stationery systems we have seen)."

There is an attempt at a certain formality here. The month is spelled out, not abbreviated. The words "AD" seem to be a stylish addition. The name of the state is written in full. Nearly all the formality is near the beginning. The letter ends with no polite wish for the reader's good health and fortune, just an appeal for money and "write as soon as tis comes to hand", which is the equivalent of John's later message of "Please write immediately."

Martinsburg is in West Virginia. This is not a mistake by William. His letter is written before West Virginia was created by the Union from the counties which broke away from the original state of Virginia during the war.

4.
Danville, Kentucky
John Huffman to George Huffman (assumed)
February 13, 1863

Ky
Hospital No. 1
3rd Division Army

Danville Feb. 13th /63

Dear Brother:
I neglected answering your letter of Dec. 18" when I ought, and than was taken down with a fever, therefore, I was unable to write. it was 4 weeks yesterday since I took sick, I had a pretty hard time of it, but am now abel to walk out in town, my health is improving fast. I expect to go to my regiment next week (if I keep improving as I have been) [John's ( ) parentheses) which is in Nashville Tenn [begin pg. 2] There are more soldiers dies of disease here than are killed in the battle field. I have been in the hospitals, here in Danville, (either sick or well) [( ) again by JJH] for the past two months and it is distrefsing to see the soldiers dying daily, there has over three hundred soldiers die in this place, since I have been here, we have had as many as three dead men in this house at once. Sometimes their wives come to see them or their brothers or Fathers, and it looks hard to see their friends die, and have no person to weep with them, or share their sorrow or speak a word of comfort to them. Sometimes they bury them here and sometimes they take the body home [last three words squeezed into a narrow margin at the page bottom]
[begin pg. 3] I know one case in which a father came to see his son, who was sick, and the son got well and the father took sick and died and another case in which a woman came to see her husband, the man got well and his wife took sick and died and I

have heard of a good many other similar circumstances. These things appear to be lamentable, but we should not lament, we should be satisfied with our lot, let it be cast where it may, we have no right to complain because every complaint we make is against or Supreme Ruler. As for my part (as you know I always am) [( ) JJH] I am perfectly happy and contented. It is true I [begin pg. 4] had a pretty hard time of it when I was sick and some of them thought I was going to wink out. but I was not the least discouraged or home-sick, I feel thankful that I am alive and my health is good as it is. I expect that you have heard the news from broth. David since I have, I have not heard from him since he left here. Hoping these few lines find you all in good health, I will close by asking you to write immediately, I don't ask it because it is fashionable, but because I want you to write.
Direct to (haven't got room) [( ) JJH] Yours Respfly JJ Huffman

[Upside down in the margin at the top of pg. 4 is the notation – "Enclosed please find five dollars"]

This letter was written five months after John Huffman enlisted. This is his first letter in the collection. There are more letters in the collection written by John than any other writer.

I believe this letter is written to an older brother, George Huffman, who remained at home in Ohio. He is referred to in later letters written by Eve Anne, Matilda, and C.J. Huffman, as well as William Bowman.

The inside address identifies John (and by extension, David) as being in the 3rd division of the "Kentucky Army". A subsequent letter refers to the "Army of The Cumberland".

While there is no state written in connection to the town of Danville, I found one in Kentucky, but none in Tennessee (making it an uncommon state in that regard). In support of a Kentucky location, I wrote a letter to the historical society in Danville, Kentucky, referencing

"Hospital No. 1". I received a quick reply stating that indeed there were several hospitals in Danville. Hospital No. 1 turned out to be a brand new county courthouse, completed just in time to be commandeered by the Union Army as a hospital. A question arises from John's comment that "we have had as many as three dead men in this house at once." Does he mean that literally? Is he in another location and not in the courthouse hospital? It is a court "house", of course, but it seems more likely that he would call it a building. Judging by the frequency of death, three deaths in such a large hospital seems like a small number.

Like William, John makes frequent and fervent reference to his religious faith. More so than William, he seems to be "witnessing" to George and any other readers of his letter; perhaps he wanted to keep them straight in their own faith.

Reception of the Ninth Indiana Volunteers at Danville, Kentucky, After Driving Out the Rebels. Drawn by Mr. H. Mosler.(Harper's Weekly, November 8, 1862)

Despite his writing that he was "...not in the least discouraged or home-sick" one wonders if this is more for the reassurance of those at home.

Like William's two earlier letters, this one is very "newsy", filled with the sorts of details of Civil War army life that we are familiar with from history books. Like those who read these letters in the 1860s, modern readers will probably find the boys' descriptions poignant, personal, and meaningful. We are learning the facts intimately, almost as if the letters were being written to us. In addition, we know the portent of what was to come.

Coming upon this letter after having read two of William Bowman's letters, the superiority of the penmanship (cursive), writing style, and spelling is immediately apparent. While there is a certain ambivalence in commas, end mark punctuation and capitalization, contractions are completely absent. John's (and later David's, as you will see) are much more legible. Until I did some research, I didn't think too much beyond this point. Part of that research was to write to the archives of the State of Indiana where the Huffman brothers enlisted. The answer I got gave me another in a series of "goose bump experiences". I described the first two of these experiences in my Foreword. These goose bumps arrived when I read that both John's and David's occupation at enlistment was "Teacher". Well, so was I! That gave me a strong connection to the two. The enlistment record lists their ages as 29 and 25, respectively. Depending on William's correct age upon his enlistment, that would make David six to ten years older, and John ten to fourteen. How did William happen to have friends so much older? I think the connection is shown by the 1860 Census which lists William as a member of the household of 80-year old Daniel Huffman, very possibly the grandfather of all the Huffman siblings who figure so prominently in the letters. William is listed as a farmhand and may be an orphan. Living with Huffman kin would make William a part of the expanded family. New Cumberland is a close-knit community which takes care of its own, whether an orphan like William, or an illegitimate child born to one of the siblings.

JIM DOHREN

I have copies of John Huffman's weekly muster roles. He is listed as "private, Co. I 85 Reg't Indiana Infantry". For September of 1862, he is shown as detached as "Hosp'l Nurse". From "Feb. 1863 and Ap'l to Oct. 1863" he is "On extra or daily duty as Regt'l Hosp'l Nurse. From "May and July 1864" he is "Absent detached at Brig. Hd. Qrs.", and from "Aug. 1864 to May 1865" he is "Absent on detached service with Brig. Ambulance Corps." So, if he were serving with the 85th Indiana almost from the beginning as a nurse, it is possible, even likely, that John contracted his fever serving others in that capacity. I have not seen David's muster roles, so I don't know if the brothers served together as nurses. David lists himself as being in Co. J, so they may not have served together that closely.

The writing paper is high quality, blue-lined stationery sizeable enough to allow a single sheet to be folded twice to give four writing surfaces. The letter is well preserved.

There is no embossed water mark. In the upper left corner the following is printed in red ink: the name "J.R. Hawley, Cin", the slogan "On to Victory, Cock-a-doodle-doo" and the engraving of a rooster.

The following words are written over or crossed out: "abel", "after" "you". It is noteworthy that John is accurate with his spelling. He has no problem with some pretty sophisticated words: *circumstances, satisfied, discouraged, immediately, fashionable.* Is he good at it, or, having slack time in the hospital, does he consult a source to check? I can't help but wonder and admire John for his ability. Not all schoolteachers of the time were so careful or skilled.

5.
Tullahoma, Tennessee
John Huffman to Anne Huffman
April 25, 1863

Tullahoma Tenn April 25th /64

Dear Sister:
Your kind epistle of no date, came to hand a few days Since and was thankfully received and careully perused. I was especially glad to hear that your health was good and that you had a good home and was well Satisfied. You will find that if you take a friend with you, that you will always have friends. Ever be ready to do a favor, and always have a kind word for every person; and above all, as virtue is the brightest jewel that ever [begin p.2] a lady was adorned with, adhere strictly to its principals. My advice to you, not to go to Indiana, need not discourage you in the least; as you are already there and well satisfied. I was only afraid you would be discontented. But I would advise you not to go to Clay co. unlefs Brother George moves out there , which I think is extremely doubtful. We are now on a march and have just camped for the night at Tullahoma Tnn about 75 miles south of Nashville. We have been marching for the last Six days. I cannot tell you where we will stop. I received your letter at Murfreesboro while on the march, but could not avail myself of an opportunity to answer it, until the present, which is a vary poor one. As your letter was not dated I could not tell how long it was on the way. I hope you will write immediately. We receive our mail while marching I hope you will remember me in your prayrs.

Your affectionate brother,

J.J. Huffman
85" Ind. Vol.

via Nashville
Tenn.

P.S. Brother David and I are
both well; and Stand
the march well. J.J.H.

Not a lot of "war news" is shared in this letter. In fact, it's not very newsy at all. Its tone is more in the area of advice and conversation between John and his sister, Anne.

From what he wrote, it's obvious that this isn't the first time Anne's moving to Indiana has come up in their correspondence. He is quite gracious when he learns that she has moved to Indiana despite his advice not to, stating "I was only afraid you would be discontented." I have an envelope in the collection with a subsequent letter addressed to "Miss Eve Anne Huffman, Middletown, Henry Co., Indiana" to support Anne's whereabouts. We don't know if John's further advice not go to Clay County, Indiana, also goes unheeded. His extreme doubts about their brother George moving out there is supported by a nearly contemporary letter (July 1864) from George's wife Matilda to Anne stating that their family is delaying any plan to move to Indiana "...until the war is over...".

The 1860 census shows that the brothers were already in Indiana living on the farm of Thomas Carrithers (73) and his wife Sarah (68). There are no others living on the farm, so it is likely that the brothers are boarding there as part of their teaching contract, a common enough practice for rural districts in the 19th century. While this does answer the question about who came to Indiana first, it does not tell us why Anne is living there away from the rest of the family. A plausible reason comes from closely reading information from the 1860 and 1880 census reports which involves a possible family scandal. In the print-out of the 1860 census report, a two-year old boy with the curious name of Leroy "d idydamath" Dolvin is listed as living with Anne, her parents, and her siblings. By now, I had become quite proficient at reading 19th century handwriting. As I enlarged the document and looked more closely at the

1860 cursive, I found that "d idydamath" could be interpreted as "illegitimate". Wow!

When I looked at the 1880 census report, I found that living with William and Anne (now Anne Bowman) and their two children Mary (9) and Jesse (7) was Martin Huffman (32), Anne's brother and Leroy Huffman (22). Is it possible that Leroy is Anne's out-of-wedlock child born when she was 18? The 1860 census shows an Isaac Dolvin (32), married and farming next to Anne's uncle. Dolvins are also mentioned in one of the letters. The same census report lists Anne living with her family, but one letter relates that she was actually staying with the Strawns before she moved to Indiana. Why is the boy with her family and not her? No mention is made of little Leroy in any of the letters. Could he be with Anne in Indiana? This explanation of Anne's residence would also explain John's concern for Anne's virtue i.e. "... above all, as virtue is the brightest jewel that ever a lady was adorned with, adhere strictly to its principals". John does seem accepting of the situation whatever it is ..."I was especially glad to hear your health was good and you had a good home and was well Satisfied".

If the child is truly Anne's, what effect would this have later on William and Anne's marriage? From his careful letters to her, we get the idea that he considers her more than just a neighbor. William must have known about Leroy, that sort of thing being almost impossible to conceal in a town as small as New Cumberland. Surely, there's little doubt that Leroy Dolvin and Leroy Huffman are the same person - one to whom the Huffman family finally gave their name. Did William accept Leroy as part of the marriage arrangement gently or grudgingly? From census records, I could surmise that William may have been an orphan with no land of his own. He is four years younger than Anne. Does their mutually weak social status draw them together? We may never know. The whole affair does speak loudly about the compassion and forgiving nature of William and the Huffman family.

This letter was written in the spring of 1864, so John and David have been enlisted for nearly 18 months. Surely, if Anne's move to Indiana preceded or even coincided with that of the boys as they went to enlist, this issue would already have been settled. With whom is she living? John's short homily on cultivating friendship is interesting. Is Anne living in Indiana with a friend? And how much can we infer from his words? Is this a hint that Anne is endangering her virtue by the nature of her residence in Indiana? Or, is this just a big brother's dutiful concern for a well-loved sister? Either way, it's a statement so stereotypical for a 19th century male that it might cause us to smile or shake our head. We can create many imaginative scenarios for Anne's behavior, but is Anne any different from the rest of the Huffman women? She has moved away from home and seems settled and happy.

Returning to the actions of a mundane schoolmaster, John seems to be chiding Anne more than just a little by twice referring to the fact that she didn't date her latest letter. Perhaps he feels that a more proper form is needed, but I'll bet he simply wants to know how long it took her to write back to him, and not just how long the letter took to reach him.

John's writing style, penmanship, and skillful mechanics are consistent with his letter from the hospital several months earlier, even though this one was written under more trying conditions ("an opportunity.... which is a vary poor one") after several days of marching, followed by setting up camp. He is also pretty inconsistent with the use of a capital "S" to begin words which are not at the beginning of a sentence. The word "satisfied" is spelled both with and without the capital "S".

As with the "Hospital No. 1" letter, this letter has only the briefest mention of David. Since we have evidence that David was writing separately to Anne, this is easily understood.

6.
Location Unknown (possibly Chickamauga)
Letter fragment
Undated (If Chickamauga, September 19-20, 1863)

Your kind favor came to hand yesterday and rec'd a hearty welcome. I was vary glad to hear that you was all well especially that Sister Matilda was recovering from her illness, for she writes me more letters than of you when she is well. You say if I get sick, and want any person to wait on me just you let you know and you will be on horses. I would say in reply, that you can no more come here than you can go to heaven in a hand basket. [begin p.2} Right now that battle is going on, and has been for sometime. Bragg while fleeing before Rosecrans got vary heavely reinforced it is supposed by Johnson and Lee both and they turned , and one of the awfulest battles is being fought, that ever was known in an open field fight. Unfortunately for us (or perhaps fortunately) [( ) JJH?] we

in the fight.
are in the reserve corps and do not have the honor of participating^ our boys are vary anxious to go forward. We have no particulars of the fight. Our loss is vary heavy

This is another letter from Jerry's collection. He comments: "Probably from John Huffman (referring to sister-in-law Mathilda [sic]) and relating to the start of the Battle of Chickamauga, which took place in both Tennessee and Georgia: Sept. 19-20, 1863.

This excerpt is only a single two-sided page which may be part of another letter, and is unidentified as to author or addressee. (PPS) This writing matches very well the writing in the letter you sent, from J.J. Huffman, 'Hospital 1 Dear brother – 2/13/63 making my letter a highly probable J.J. Huffman, as well.'The single page is very badly weathered (dark brown stains and blotches, written on unlined paper, in what appears to be brown ink). The page appears to be

The Battle of Chickamauga

the bottom 6 inches of a larger page (5 x 8) since the first line is only half a word high."

I think Jerry is right in believing this to be a fragment of a longer letter. There's the evidence which he has stated. In addition, I can add that there is no inside address, no closing signature identifying the writer, and no return address. These details are found in all of the other letters. I would also agree with Jerry that this fragment probably refers to fighting involved in the Battle of The Chickamauga. I have only Jerry's transcription of this letter.

It is interesting to speculate about what happened to the probable other half of the letter. I certainly didn't get it with my batch of letters. One strong clue is its bad condition. Since I have not seen it, I have no idea how bad it is. The conditions of the letters in my collection all seem to be better than this one. Only one or two have stains and blotches. Certainly, they are all complete. A good first guess would be that the letter was damaged after being received, the first part beyond salvage. If that's the case, the very fact that the less damaged part was saved speaks volumes about how precious these letters were to those who collected and guarded them. I suppose an expert could test the paper to come up with the nature of the stains and determine when the damage might have occurred.

Even though there is no inside address or date, Jerry accounts for this when he describes the first line as being only a half a word high. The missing information would have been the beginning of the letter. The narrative flows logically in what remains which is likely the middle of the letter.

That "Matilda" (or "Mathilda", as Jerry writes) was George Huffman's wife is established in other letters sent to Anne from the women in the Huffman family as well as those that she received from friends. Both spellings of her name appear in them. Jerry may be right as to which Matilda this is written about; however, John also has a sister named Matilda.

In Jerry's transcription of this partial letter, he follows the writer's phrase '...than you can go to heaven in a hand basket.' with the comment "And we thought was a newly turned phrase." I would add that many expressions which we think are of recent vintage are much older. And, expressions that we assume died out when we stopped being kids, are actually still in use today. In the 21st century, the threat of one "going to hell in a hand basket" is so mildly stated that it is hardly utilized. I wonder if that more sinister version was known back then and just turned around by (assumedly) John Huffman.

A Civil War scholar would know about the 85th Indiana being kept in reserve. Did it finally get into the fight? Since the Huffmans were in the ambulance corps, I wonder if they weren't moved up to help with the terrible casualties.

Since this letter is written seven months after his previous one in the collection, John is almost certainly reunited with David, though he doesn't mention him. That is not really significant when only half the letter exists. David may well have been mentioned in the missing half.

7.
Fosterville, Tennessee
David Huffman to Anne Huffman
November 20, 1863

Fosterville, Temm Nov. 20" /63
Mifs E. A. Huffman
Dear sister
I seat myself this rainy evening for the purpose of addrefsing you with a few lines in answer to your kind epistle which I received a few days since. I have nothing new to write so I will tell you the old tale, We are in camp at Fosterville, We have been here two weeks longer than we have staid at one place for some time. We may remain here for a while if the rebs stays out of Tenn., But if they make a raid we will have to travel again to keep them from destroying the railroad. We are fixed for living here if we remain we have homes built with chimneys to them and are living at the top of the pot. There has not any Snow fell yet, it has rained considerable the last month But the weather has been very pleasant for this season of the year. Evrything appears to be quite calm at present the army appears to be lying Still. There is always a calm before a storm so look out for news. [begin p.2] We have plenty of hard tack, Coffee, Sugar, beans and Sow belly to eat so there is no danger of us starving. I should not be surprised if we had a mefs of fresh pork once in a while and a chicken for breakfast on Sunday morning as long as there is anything in Tenn, the soldiers will live well. It is raining very hard and they are bring ing in clothing for the Soldiers so I will close Brother John & I are both well and I hope these few lines will find you all well.

I will close hoping to hear from you Soon.
Yours truly,
D.L. Huffman
Co. J[?] 85 Regt
Ind. Vol Inft

Via Nashville
Tenn

This is an altogether interesting letter. There's a lot to speculate about with this one, beginning with the fact that it's the only letter from David in the collection. Why aren't there more of David's letters? In fact, considering that the letters cover a span of more than two years, it seems a sparse output of correspondence in general. One reason is that all of these letters came from those kept by Eve Anne Bowman (nee Huffman). The boys would presumably have written many letters to others. Were these all that Anne received?

Records from the National Archives provide one solid reason why David did not write during three months of 1863. He was a prisoner captured on March 5 at Thompson's Station, Tennessee. The records show he was quickly exchanged (March 31) at City Point, Virginia, and the next day was at Camp Parole, Maryland. From there, he was processed through Camp Chase, Ohio (April 13), and Camp Morton, Indiana (April 21), before returning to the regiment in Franklin, Tennessee on June 10. The system of prisoner exchange or "parole", as it was called, was especially valued by the Confederacy as it largely eliminated the need to use scarce resources of food and medical supplies for prisoners when they could hardly supply their own men and guard personnel. A vital component of the parole system was an agreement adhered to by both sides that paroled soldiers could not be returned to combat. This did indirectly help the combat forces, of course, by allowing paroled soldiers to take the place of able bodied men serving in rear echelon positions or as nurses and ambulance drivers on the front lines. The exchange system was a sensible one and humane when it worked as smoothly and quickly as it did for David. However, when the system broke down, it could be an insurmountable problem for the South as witnessed by the disgraceful nightmare of Andersonville Prison.

The knowledge of David's capture and parole answers another question as well, and that is why John was in the ambulance corps. David does not list it as part of his return address in his letter written after his return to the 85th. John does note the ambulance corps in his letters, so it's not unreasonable to surmise that John transferred there because that's where David was. It's curious that David's capture, repatriation, and return to the regiment are never mentioned in any of John's letters.

Another reason that David's letter is interesting is how formal he is in his writing style. He does not write to "Dear Sister" but to "Miss E.A. Huffman". He closes with "Yours Truly" in contrast to John's "Your affectionate brother". Why? In what he writes, though, David is just as mundane (and newsy, thank goodness) as John. Is David just more of a stickler for form, or is there something else? Could this indicate that there is a rift between Anne and David caused by problems that she is blamed for in bearing an illegitimate child? If that is so, and David was more rigid than John, then this letter may be the only one Anne received from him, and therefore all the more important.

With only one letter from David as an example, it is perhaps unjust to make the observation that he makes no reference to religious principal which often, and strongly, appear in the letters of John and William. If he gives Anne no words of comfort, at least he doesn't preach to her either.

It is certainly an informative letter, despite its brevity, with many details of infantry life. David's mention of "... a mefs of fresh pork once in a while and a chicken for breakfast on Sunday morning as long as there is anything in Tenn. the soldiers will live well" is an obvious reference to the foraging the Union farm boys were so adept at in Confederate territory. David seems perfectly comfortable in describing it.

David crossed out the word "there" and didn't write over any words. His spelling, grammar, and usage are excellent and better than his older brother's, although he does use a capital "S" in some strange places. Was this a custom of the time, or an idiosyncrasy of the writer? It's doubtful, but since it is so short, could this be a second draft of the letter? As with John's earlier letter, David writes an "ss" as "fs". That had been standard usage during that time.

Curiously, he neglects to do this when addressing his letter to Mi<u>ss</u> E. A. Huffman.

In my original transcription, I copied Co. "J" for David's outfit. In John's muster reports, it is clearly written that he was in Co. "I". I may have misread what David wrote and accidentally put him in a different company.

Unlike most of the letters, this one was written on two pages only. A neat tear along the left edge of the paper suggests it came from a tablet that David may have carried. The paper is blue-lined. There is a water mark of the Mt. Holly Paper Co. in the upper left corner of this letter. The letter has damage from water or another substance. Some small parts are faded and barely legible.

Like all the others, this letter was folded several times to fit into a small envelope such as the ones included in the collection. Making the envelope so small to save space in the post is reminiscent of the World War II miniaturization known as V-mail.

8.
Kingston, Georgia
John Huffman to Anne Huffman
May 22, 1864

May 22" 1864

Dear Sister:
I received your kind letter day before yesterday. and was quite glad to hear from you, especially to hear that you was enjoying good health: and when these few lines reaches you. they will still find you enjoying the same blessing. Brother David and I are still blesfsed with good health, but we have endured considerable hardships in the way of fighting and marching, since last I wrote you. I will not pretend to describe to you what we have done, for it would be uselefs; besides you will have it in the papers long [begin pg. 2] before this reaches you. We are now In georgia near Kingston. We have halted here, to wrest a day or two; and then we expect to resume our journey. Save yesterday, and to day, we have not been from under the sound of the Cannon, for the last two weeks. We have not done very much hard fighting, but have been skirmishing considerable. The rebs are in full retreat and it is unknown to us, where they will make the next stand. We belong to the Twentieth Corps commanded by Gen. Hooker. This Country looks very desolate; more than half of the dwellings being evacuated. On the evening of the 19" a portion of our Brigade made a charge on Cass-vill and [begin pg 3] took the place, the rebs leaving in confusion. Our soldiers fared sumtuously on suppers prepared for the rebs; besides bacon, tobacco, sugar and molasses; which came in vary good play, for our boy was hungry and tired. we expect to leave this place tomorrow, but I don't know where we will go. You ask my advice about going with the

family you now <the word "now" added between lines> live with; I will give you none; do as you think best.

Please write son
Your affectionate
Brother
J.J. Huffman
Co. I 85[t"] Regt Ind Vol
2" Brig. 3" Div. 20" A.C.
Army of the Cumberland

Kingston is in the northeast corner of Georgia, not too far from Rome, on a line from Chattanooga to Atlanta. Cassville is a town about five miles due east of Kingston.

I wonder what the "considerable hardships in fighting and marching" were. These may well be euphemisms to avoid frightening the folks at home or to generalize and thus save writing time and space. Since the Huffman brothers are not given to easy complaining, I assume the conditions may have been pretty harsh. One hint is given later in the letter when John writes "our boy(s) was hungry and tired". Being hungry and tired is a pretty mild complaint for any soldier in any war, but still. If he was grammatically accurate, maybe John is personalizing when he writes "our boy was hungry and tired."

Again, we have a reference to the accepted practice of the army foraging for supplies while in rebel territory. Even John, the man of strong Christian principle, professes no qualms. "Our soldiers feasted sumtuously on suppers prepared for the rebs; besides bacon, tobacco, sugar and molasses; which came in vary good play..." This activity became an especially vital one after Sherman cut his army from its supply train on its movements from Atlanta to Savannah, the renowned March to the Sea.

General Hooker had a disastrous and short career as commander of The Army of The Potomac. Ironically, he was in this position during the Battle of The Wilderness in which William was captured.

We have evidence contained in this letter that Anne has been living with a family. We can't tell if this is the first person or family she's stayed with in Indiana. Unlike in his other letters, John no longer makes the effort nor takes the space to give his sister advice. He just acknowledges the truth of the matter; Anne will do as she wishes. We can also wonder if she is seeking and getting advice from David as well.

This is the most complete return address on any of the letters so far. The return address is also noteworthy because it is the first time John includes the notation "20" A.C." for 20th Ambulance Corps. We have a record from the summary of his brigade roster that he was in the ambulance corps from August 1864 through May 1865. From May through July of 1864, he was "detached at Brig. Hd. Qrs." i.e. brigade headquarters. As part of that detachment, he must therefore have already been assigned to ambulance duty. It's interesting to speculate if this was volunteer duty on John's part. We have learned of his strong religious faith, so in all likelihood, this is a job he sought.

There is an abandonment of John's habit of capitalizing an "S" when it doesn't begin a sentence. There is also an inconsistency in the treatment of double "s"; i.e. "blessing, blesfed, useless. This could be easily explained if he were rushed and stressed, a likely possibility if the march was as he described.

On a folded section of the letter is the notation "wrote to Mrs. Wm. Bowman. Jesse's mother" It is followed by the initials "L.D." All of this is in pencil or badly faded ink. Who is this "Jesse"? And whose initials are "L.D.'s"? Here is my surmise. In my notes and comments for the second letter that William wrote from Parkersburg, Virginia, I noted that after the war Anne Huffman and William Bowman were married. They had three children - two daughters and a son. One girl died in infancy, but their son, whom they named Jesse (called "Jess") lived 102 years. In fact, I met him a couple of times on my early visits to Ohio. Jesse Bowman married my Grandfather Daugherty's youngest sister, Rebecca, making her and Jesse my mother's great uncle and aunt (her favorites, she always said). One of Rebecca Daugherty's brothers was Hugh Daugherty's grandfather and Lillian Daugherty's father-in-law. Got

Arrival of Union Refugees at Kingston, Georgia.- .Sketched by Theodore R. Davis. Harper's Weekly December 10, 1864.

that? So, I think Lillian wrote a message on the back of this letter long after it was written to let anyone interested know that it was sent to Anne Huffman Bowman, "Jesse's mother". I'm glad she didn't feel she needed to do this on all the letters.

The maker's mark on this paper is a crest with no discernible lettering. The paper is heavy stock, blue-lined, and folded in the familiar stationery form.

9.
Camp Sumter, Georgia
William Bowman to David Huffman
June 2, 1864

June the 2 1864
Camp Sumter georgia

Mr. David Huffman
Dear Friend
it is with pleasure that I seat my sealf this morning to let you know that I am well and hearty and to let you know that I am a prisioner I was captured on the evening of the sixth of May and they have used us middling well since we have been prisioners I was captured in the wilderness close to the rapadan on the second days fight I have not got anny thing more to write at preasant sow I will close good by
[on reverse]
William Bowman
Prisioner of War

This is the shortest letter of the collection, but certainly one of the most ominous. The reason is not just that William is a prisoner-of-war, but what prison he is in. It took a good deal of research to discover that Camp Sumter, a name honoring the battle which began the Civil War, was only temporary as the prison camp was supposed to be. Soon the camp name evolved to that of the nearby village – Andersonville. The horrors of Andersonville Prison are very well known and documented. Major Wirtz, the commandant at Andersonville, was the only Confederate tried for his crimes after the war. He was convicted and hung.

The hellhole that was Andersonville Prison caused abysmal suffering for the prisoners. There were several reasons for the conditions at Andersonville. The greatest reason was probably the breakdown of the prisoner exchange system between the Confederate and Union

Union prisoners at Andersonville, GA.

forces. The practice of exchanging prisoners was an old one. As stated previously, it spared each side the expense, effort, and responsibility of guarding and humanely caring for thousands of men. It had worked reasonably well until General Grant determined that it benefited the Confederacy considerably more than the Union. Grant's overall strategic plan was fundamental - fight a war of attrition; bleed the South dry of soldiers. Prisoners the Union exchanged were much more likely to rejoin their regiments than Union soldiers, thus prolonging the struggle. Despite the fact that the abysmal conditions of prisons like Andersonville and Libby Prison were known, Grant was adamant and held out against immense popular and political pressure to relent. The Union ended prisoner exchanges for months until they no longer mattered in the final outcome. The Confederates, who were woefully weak in supplying food and medicine to their own troops, were utterly overwhelmed by the build-up of tens of thousands of prisoners. All the while, its own regiments were thinning due to combat casualties, and losses of men due to the interplay of malnutrition, infection, and disease brought on by the scarcities. In other words, despite its Draconian aspects, Grant's policy worked. It would be truly unjust not to note that prisoners in Union prisons hardly fared better. Conditions in Camp Douglas in Illinois, to name one, were only marginally better than those in some prisons. When one factors in the advantages of food, medicine, and manpower available to the North, one has a tendency to believe the adage that the victors write the history books.

So, how then did William come to be exchanged before he succumbed to conditions at Andersonville? The answer lies in the fact that the Confederates were so overwhelmed by Andersonville that they desperately offered to exchange prisoners at well beyond the normal complicated formulas of how many enlisted men were equal to an officer or even a simple one-for-one exchange. In late November of 1864, 13,000 Andersonville inmates were exchanged for 3,000 Confederates in Savannah. A repeat of this arrangement took place on January 24, 1865. Since William was reported in the postwar roster of the 126th Ohio as a paroled prisoner at Camp Chase, Ohio, on March 18, 1865, it is likely that he was part of the second exchange. The great probability was that few, if any, of these men were even close to being considered effective soldiers. William certainly wasn't.

One can't help but compare William's ordeal as a prisoner-of-war with David Huffman's which occurred earlier. David was exchanged within three weeks of his capture, moved swiftly through the system, and was back with his regiment (and brother) in about 90 days. That's about as efficiently as the official parole system worked. Only the unofficial, impromptu exchanges arranged by enemy commanders immediately after a battle worked more quickly. If David was lucky, it was ironically.

William is quite laconic in his announcement of being a prisoner and being captured in the Battle of The Wilderness. For obvious reasons, he could say little of the terrible fighting, and he had not yet experienced what he was to suffer at Andersonville. He was probably just grateful to have a chance to truthfully write that he was still alive and unwounded. Add that to the fact that later records show that he also spent time in the infamous Libby Prison in Richmond, Virginia. Life there would have taught him that the less said the better if he wanted his letter to make it home. It makes me wonder why he wrote to David about his status. Had he read that David had also been a prisoner-of-war? It's possible chronologically. How many letters was he able to write from prison compounds? Surely, not many. There are certainly no others in the collection.

After the war, William applied twice for a government disability pension. His first in 1888, based on a claim that his feet were crippled by '... wearing too short shoes" was denied. I have a copy of an increase in his approved second application from the Bureau of Pensions dated May 19, 1909, stating, "This pension being for rheumatism and resulting irritable heart (as a) result of prison life". (Could he have contracted rheumatic fever in prison?) The second application was accompanied by a record of a doctor's examination. My mother told me she remembered seeing William as an old, old man in the 1920's. His fingers and toes were so knotted and curled in upon themselves that he could barely walk or use his hands. He was in constant pain.

This letter was written on paper that looks as if it were torn in two. Maybe prisoners had to share paper, or maybe this is the allotment they were given. The only writing on the back side of the paper is William's closing, so he had space to write more, but didn't. Certainly he was limited in what he was allowed to write. I doubt that letters from prison were sent home uncensored. It is somewhat of a small miracle that this letter made it home at all. It also begs the question of how it came to be in Anne's collection if it was written to David. Most likely it was in David's effects which were given to John, then to Anne, when he returned to Indiana. The letter is pretty much unblemished and easy to read. Unfortunately, over the years it has been folded and refolded many times causing it to separate into two pieces at one of the folds.

Interestingly, the regimental record that I obtained from the Bureau of Archives shows that from April 18 to September 5, 1863, the 126th was detached for duty in New

Andersonville prison seen from the guard tower, Andersonville, Georgia, 1864 (Gilder Lehrman Collection)

York City to help quell the draft riots there. I wonder what the Ohio farm boy thought of that. No letter exists, so we have no way of ever knowing.

I wrote to the Andersonville Prison National Historic Site asking them if they had any record of William being there. I was disappointed when they answered that they did not. However, when I made a visit there in 2004, I looked up William Bowman on the computerized record and found, sure enough, that he was listed as a prisoner. At the end of the brief record, it simply said "Survived".

10.
New Cumberland, Ohio
Ruth Davy to Anne Huffman
June 6, 1864

New Cumberland
Ohio

Monday June 6th AD 64

Dear Friend,
I seat myself this afternoon to write you a few lines in answer to your kind letter that came to hand about two weaks ago. I expect you began to think that I wasn't agoing to answer a tall but the reason I did not write was because I did not feel like it. I was not verry well. I had the toothache about three weeks and I had something like the scarlet rash. I was very sick with it nearly every body around here has had it, but I feel pretty nigh strait again, onily I am a little tired the rest of the family is well and the health of our neighborhood (pg. 2) is very good at the present. (Criss) and (Til) [Ruth's parentheses] was here yesterday a lttle while and they were all well. We went up to Davids (Huffman ?) in the evening to prayer meeting and their was agreat many their. The house was full, and we had a verry good meeting.
The girls and David take it very hard about Billy sense the word came that he is missing The poor fellow it is hard to tell wheather he is taken prisoner or killed
I received a letter from Wesley a few days ago he stated he came through the battle safe and was well when he wrote we had a great many brave soldiers that fell in that battle they say it was the hards battle than has bin (pg.3)
This is wednesday evening and we are all well. I will try and finish my letter but I haven't mustch time. I want to take it to the office to night there is alot of youngsters agoing up to town to a singing to night I wish you was here to go with us for we would have

a good time they have singing their every wednesday night.
I was at a big sewing last Thursday at Mrs. Strawns their was just twenty fourold women and girls all together took supper their we had a very plesent time of it
Well, I must bring my letter to a close for this time excuise me for not writing sooner I will try to do better the next time (pg 4)
I wish I was out their with you I bet that we would have a big time I often think of the times we ust to have when you lived at Strawns
I must quit you must write as soon as this come to hand and I will try and answer sooner excuise my bad writing for I am in a hurry good by. write soon

From a friend
Ruth J. Davy
Ann Huffman

I will send you a peace of my new dress

This is one of the letters that Jerry sent to me. In his notes he states, "half-folded 8-1/2" X 10"' with circular maker's mark with DOVE in center. Brown ink – nearly all vertically double-stroked letters, such as 'l, t, d, etc.' were blobbed (run together) due to nearness of the lines and runniness of the ink. Reference to Billy (William Bowman) and Wes Hoopingarner."

This is another "newsy" letter, just what people then (and now) wish to read. It's a nicely preserved letter, too, so it's quite easy to read even the copy. Only the seams that were created by folding cause problems.

Ruth writes "We went up to David's ... in the evening." After the word "David's" she squeezes in something which looks like "Huffman. Who would that David Huffman be? Levi is the father of George, David, John, Anne and the other Huffman siblings. However, there is a neighbor, David Huffman, who is surely their uncle with whom William lived and worked before the war. He and his wife, who may be named either Cristina or Catherine, and their children, live in Rose Township, so are close neighbors to the Levi Huffman family. Their children are close enough in age to the Huffmans and Davys to make it sensible to have a prayer meeting at their home. According to the 1860 census, Daniel Huffman, age 80, the Huffman siblings' grandfather, is also living with David, his wife and children, and William.

Was it accepted practice to put nicknames in parentheses then, or is it just something Ruth does? The "Criss" is Christiana Huffman, the "Til" is Matilda Huffman, probably the one who is Anne's sister, not her sister-in-law.

The battle referred to is surely the Battle of the Wilderness for it's the one in which William was captured and where the 126th suffered so many casualties.

There are several references to social gatherings – a sewing circle, a prayer meeting, and a sing-a-long. There appeared to be a lot of homemade entertainment and mutual support during hard times. Certainly the war would have been a cause of constant conversation.

Ruth's comment that she wishes she were with Anne in Indiana makes me wonder if she was just missing a good friend, or if it was admiration and some envy for Anne's separating herself from the old hometown.

Ruth gives evidence that Anne lived with a different family, the Strawns, and not with her own family before she moved to Indiana. She begs forgiveness for her "bad writing", but she does rather well remembering the "i before e" rule when she correctly spells "received" and "neighborhood", and even gets "Wednesday" and "toothache" right. Ruth writes three times that she is about to end her letter, yet she keeps writing. She may really be rushed as she says, but it's interesting to speculate that she just keeps thinking of things Anne would like to read.

The "office" she refers to is certainly the New Cumberland post office.

Presuming the "Wesley" who Ruth refers to when she writes that "... he came through the battle safe and was well when he wrote" is Wes Hoopingarner. One is struck by his disingenuousness since we know he deserted the Union Army to get out of Andersonville Prison - if he indeed had made the decision to do so at the time he wrote. If not, and he was still a prisoner-of-war, why didn't he write that as William had?

11.
New Cumberland, Ohio
Matilda Huffman to Anne Huffman
July 14, 1864

/64
New Cumberland Ohio July the 14

Miss Anne Huffman

Dear sister
I rect your kind and welcomed letter in due time after it was wrote but have not answerd it for George was very sick when I got the letter so you will pardon me for not writing George had a hard spell of bilious fever he lay in the doctors hands for two weeks he was to me out of his head a part of the time it was a great pleasure^ that I could be with him in time of sickness and take care of him how many women are deprived of that priviliege their husbands are in far distant lands George is able to work again but not very stout yet our girls are almost big they are great company and help to me when their pa is gone for he is gone every day when he is able he is working for Dolvin again this summer he gets one dollar per day we have the prettiest and smartest and best children in our parts but not, many of them as you know Mary went to school six mounths and only mist one day Maggy mist several days she was sick we have a good garden this summer our cabbage is a heading very nice we have plenty of beans and cucumbers we have a nice lot of sweet potatoes[begin pg.2] You wanted to know something about the 126 reg – well I can't tell you much about them Bill Bowman is prisnor he is in the reb hands (poor Bill) {( ) by Matilda} Nick and Wes was well the last we heard poor Eli Barrick was shot in the head and his body was burnt up (O my) {( ) by M.H.}Lewis Beamer had his left arm shot off but he is getting along fine [here a line is skipped and upside down in

the space left are the words "Anne send me your photograph"]
I must begin again Pete Hoop [?] brought me a letter from John him and brother David was both well when he wrote the letter Pete got a letter from Wes I read it he was well and harty and Nick was well there is great excitement hear the report is the rebs is within six miles of the capital there is talk of a draft I fear I will haft to give up my husband O mercy what would I do old aunt polly Huffman has gone crazy about Bill some times she knows what she is doing but the most of the time she is raven She is an awful looking sight you wanted to know wether we were going to Clay co. next fall George says we are not going until the war is over and then we will go if our family is not to big I am willing to go where ever he goes and stay where ever he stays where ever he stays [repetition of the last phrase sic] I will close write soon your sister Matilda Huffman

There is an enjoyable amount to speculate about in this letter. It's fascinating just because it does not come from a soldier.

It is, of course, a "home front" letter. In fact, Matilda has so much to write about home that there is added writing on almost all the margins of the letter. She could just have started a new sheet of paper. We might correctly think of her wanting to conserve, but it's more fun to see her adding these tidbits just before folding the letter to send. We have more of Matilda's home front letters than those from any other writer.

This is about as "newsy" as a letter can be. In her nice cameo descriptions of rural life, her local war news, and the inclusion of her fears and feelings, Matilda bears out just what we have read about that time. The letter has a truly personal feel to it. It's certainly different than the letters the boys write. That's easily understandable because it seems by nature men are more taciturn than women. Add to that the fact that the soldiers self-censored their letters to keep from worrying the folks back home and because they experienced terrors that no words could describe. These limitations to letters home from the battlefields have been repeated ever since warriors began writing them. By contrast, Matilda is anxious to leave nothing out for she knows how Anne hungers for news. In those days, letters were anxiously awaited, read and re-read, shared and treasured.

Matilda writes "dear sister", though she and Anne are sisters-in-law. This is quite understandable considering that Matilda is 24 when she writes this letter, only a couple of years older than Anne, so they are obviously close friends and confidants.

We learn quite a bit about older brother George Huffman to whom at least one letter was written. For instance, we learn that he works for "Dolvin". The Dolvin who is their neighbor is Isaac Dolvin, also a carpenter like George. He's also the man who I speculatively named as the father of Anne's son Leroy Dolvin. If that's true, it makes Leroy living with George's parents all the more curious.

Matilda writes "we have the prettiest and smartest and best children in our parts but not many of them as you know". Does she mean her Mary and Maggy are the prettiest, smartest and best, and that she (Matilda) does not have many children? Or, that all the children are that way, or that there are just not many children in the local area? I am inclined toward the former. When this letter is written, Mary was nine and Maggy (Margaret) seven. Another girl, Ruth, will be born the next year and mentioned in Matilda's later letters to Anne.

Matilda uses virtually no capital letters or end mark punctuation to show separations between sentences. On the original letter this is not as confusing as it seems in print.

Her words at the paragraph break where she begins "I must begin again" makes it likely that Matilda was called away from her letter and had to come back to finish it.

Matilda spells Anne's name with an "e". In other letters her name is spelled "Ann", and in at least one letter, she is referred to as "E.A. Huffman" (for Eve Anne Huffman).

This is the letter referred to earlier as a corroboration of John's writing to Anne that George's family moving to Clay County, Indiana, is unlikely.

William Bowman is referred to as "Bill" by Matilda. Her emotional comment "poor Bill" makes me think that he was an especially close friend of the Huffmans. Perhaps Matilda had either known him as a friend before her marriage to George, or had come to like him very much afterwards. We can even speculate that she is so concerned because she knows how Anne feels about William ("Bill"). It's no wonder "old Aunt Polly Huffman has gone crazy about Bill".

The gruesome death of Eli Barrick likely occurred in the famous Battle of The Wilderness in which William was captured. It happened not too long before this letter (May 1864). In that battle, the dry woods were set afire by the fighting and many soldiers, including the helpless wounded, were burned alive. We can hope that with a head wound, Eli was not alive, or at least not conscious at the time. I have an alphabetical list summarizing the record of each of the soldiers in the 126th Ohio. William Bowman is listed with the "Bs", but Eli Barrick is not.

I believe the Pete "Hoop" that Matilda writes as having brought her a letter from John is actually a shortened name for Pete Hoopingarner. In consideration of what William writes in April of 1865, it is ironic that Matilda relates that in Wes's letter he "... was well and harty". I suppose it could be a different Wes. This is the same Pete Hoopingarner whose infant dies and who succumbs to typhoid fever himself. Pete is 26. It makes one wonder why he isn't serving. He is the head of his household and may have paid a bonus to avoid serving, like George who is 34.

Another interesting allusion is the one Matilda makes about the report of the rebs being within six miles of the capital. I was mystified by this until, while re-editing another letter and consequently making a closer reading of the casualty list of the 126th, I saw that men were killed or wounded at the Battle of Monacacy, Maryland. The events of that battle coincide perfectly with Matilda's comment about the threat to the capital. In July of 1864, Jubal Early had moved his army past Fredericksburg on the road to Washington, D.C. A desperate delaying action was conducted by outnumbered troops under General Lew Wallace. The hastily assembled Federals fought tenaciously, and while they suffered terrific casualties, they inflicted them as well. The hardest fighting was on the Union left flank where a stout defense allowed an orderly retreat back toward Washington instead of a rout. In that battle, the 126th Ohio was heavily involved and greatly praised for its steadfast courage. The 126th was in the VI Corps under General Rickets in the 3rd Division, 2nd Brigade, commanded by Lieutenant Colonel A.W. Ebright. The full day of delay, and the exhaustion that the costly battle caused the Confederates, enabled the Union to reinforce the city's defenses to the point where Early indeed did get within six miles of the capital city before withdrawing his forces, which were now inadequate for a lengthy siege. Matilda's letter is written only three days after the battle. She must have known of the location of the 126th, so she has double reason for concern.

12.
Atlanta, Georgia
John Huffman to Anne Huffman
September 11, 1864

Atlanta, Ga Sept 11" /64

Dear Sister,
Your kind letter of the 14" ultimo[?] is at hand. I was very glad to hear that you was well and well satisfyed. I hope you will do well. Brother David and I are both blessed with good health. You will already have heard that Atlanta has fallen. Gen. Sherman moved his army in the rear of Atlanta, and cut the R.R. This is what might be called one of Sherman's brilliant flank movements. He entirely destroyed Hoods communications [begin pg. 2] and greatly surprised him Hood endeavored to cut his way through our lines, but finding that impossible, he got out the best way he could. In getting out Sherman cut his army in two, and completely routed him. The rebs left Atlanta in utter confusion. We killed wounded and captured a good many of them. The Northern part of Atlanta is entirely ruined. There is hardly a house in that part of the city, but what is riddled with our cannon balls. There was several women and children killed wounded The Sitizens dug holes in the ground to live in to keep from being killed from our shells. Gen. Sherman notified Gen. Hood that he was going to shell the city and requested him to remove the women and children, but he refused to do it and did not even inform them of shermans intention. There are a good number of women and children in the city, but vary few who are able to bear arms, and they got away from the rebs in the skedaddle. All citizens have to leave the city. All families whose male representatives are in the Confederate Army or gone South are required to go South. The others can go north or south as they like. This part of the army is completely whiped and I

Atlanta burning.

think this rebellion will play out in lefs than Twelve months. It may be that the Indiana soldiers will come home to vote this fall. [begin pg. 4] I will close; Hoping these few lines will find you blefsed with good health and trusting in God for his grace.

Your
affectionate brother
J.J. Huffman
address
Ambulance Corps
2nd Brig. 3" Div. 20 A.C.
Atlanta, Ga.

This letter in the collection is unusual because it deals with the tactics of the generals instead of the life of the volunteer soldiers. John's indignation with General Hood's failure to evacuate or even warn the citizens of Atlanta of the impending bombardment is obvious. So much for Southern chivalry and honor, he seems to be saying.

I first saw "Gone With The Wind" when I was a small boy – in a re-issue I hasten to add. As an adolescent I read the entire novel in one long, captivated day. Now, both the visual and literary images charge my memory when I read John's anger in relating the siege of Atlanta, especially that the citizens, abandoned and helpless, were forced to dig "holes in the ground" to survive the shelling.

The pride the soldiers feel in what they have accomplished, in not only defeating the Confederates, but also in out-maneuvering them, is apparent. In so many earlier battles, the opposite had been the case for the Army

Sherman's March to the Sea

of The Cumberland. John refers to a “rebellion”, not a war, just as President Lincoln did.

John is only 50-50 in his predictions. He is correct in predicting the end of the war within a year, but the “Indiana soldiers” did not “...come home to vote this fall”. Instead, the 85th Indiana and the rest of Sherman’s army, cut itself off from its supply lines and disappeared into the heart of Georgia. It was not heard of again until December, when it emerged victorious at Savannah.

This letter is consistent with John’s other letters in style, penmanship, spelling, and grammar. By now, he is making scant reference to religious faith in his letters.

Why is this letter the first one in which John fails to note in his return address that he is part of the 85th Indiana Volunteers? Does he now feel part of a tighter-knit group? In his previous letters, he identifies himself as being in the “Army of The Cumberland”. Does he now first consider himself part of the 2nd Brigade, Third Division?

This letter was found in a 3” X 5” envelope addressed to “Miss Ann Huffman” and not “E.A. Huffman” as on some of the inside addresses of the letters in the collection. Her name appears without a final “e”, and the honorific is spelled as shown, not “Mifs”. The mailing address written is “Middleton, Indiana” with the addition of “Henry Co.” in the lower center of the envelope. At the time, there were two Middletowns in Indiana in 1864. Today, the Middletown in Henry County is not a very big town, but still the second largest in the county. There is no stamp on the envelope, but there is remnant of mucilage where a stamp would have been found.

In the upper left corner of this paper is an embossed maker’s mark as was found on most of the letters. This one has the letters “G&T” within a fancy border. The paper is the blue-lined paper so often used. I wonder if it was government issued. Two other possibilities arise. First, John may have purchased the paper from a “sutler”, a merchant who followed the troops to sell sundries. Second, states and private citizens often funded “Sanitary Commissions” which followed their volunteer regiments to provide them with supplies not provided by the military. I wonder if this deep in the South either of these organizations would have been working.

13.
New Cumberland, Ohio
Matilda Huffman to Anne Huffman
Sept. 28, 1864

New Cumberland O
Sept the 28 1864
Miss Anne Huffman

Kind sister
I will try and write you a few lines in answer to your kind and most welcomed letter which I rect four week ago and was glad to hear from you but was very busy and neglected to write ontil now as I am entirely alone I will chat with you a little while for company I came from Peter Hoops this morning they have had a very cerious time I doutless you have heard (pg.2)
of their sickness so I will just tell you that the babe four weeks old will not live till knight Seys is a little better but not out of danger Maryon was very bad both doctors gave him up and sayed he must dye but he got better but it is worse again Pete is well but his father is very poorly your mother has got better we are all well George is a working a B Mangun's house he offered to go as a substitute I fear he will go he gave twenty five (pg 3)
dollars to clear our own tp (township) of a draft and now will go for rose (Rose township) big Charley Scott is drafted and bob madon Jim herren their was fifty too drafted out of rose
I will close and go to Hoops for they need me do not do a I done but write soon and I will try and do better next time your sister

Matilda Huffman
29 I closed my letter yesterday but I will write a few lines this morning and tell you (pg 4) pete's babe died last knight its buryed today they meet at the house a one oclock One more saint in

glory Oh that I could have went at its age but Gods will be done

A word for our little girls dear aunt we often think and talk about you but cant see you but we got the patches of your dress and think it pretty we are a going to send you patches of our dresses the spoted is of the skirts and the plain of the waists goodby aunty

Mary and Maggie Huffman

Our little girls are allmost big and the best looking in our township one favors their mother and the other their auntie anne please write soon and I will answer (written upside down on top of pg. 2)

This is another of Jerry's letters. His comments are: "half-folded 8X10" Faint blue lines maker's mark of crest with garlands beneath. News of the draft from Rose Township (52 men) the ability to buy or serve for money to satisfy the draft quota. She always comments very positively on the looks of her daughters, and of her sister."

This is a well-preserved letter. Matilda's handwriting is, if not artistic, at least very legible other than a few strike-outs.

Another reason is given for a long delay in returning one of Anne's letters and see another variation of the spelling of Anne's name.

A familiar tragedy unfolds in this letter - an infant death. Obviously, this was a constant and real fear for parents in those days. No wonder Matilda thinks so much of her own little girls. The child's burial is immediate. There was no science and little ceremony in the death of a child then in rural America. Matilda mentions the health of Anne's mother. Her name is Mary Margaret Huffman (nee Tressel). The Tressels are close neighbors of the Huffmans. She is 57 when this letter is written.

What is behind the wish by Matilda that she could have died as an infant? It is a striking and unexpected statement to be sure, but there seem to be no clues here or in other letters to help us speculate.

The “Seys” mentioned near the top of the second page is probably short for “Cecil”. I remember an uncle by that nickname on Mom’s side when I was a boy.

Perhaps it only seems to me as if fifty-two men gone in the draft seems like a lot for a rural township, but it surely did make for many hardships.

At the close of her letter, Matilda writes rather touchingly in pretending to be her daughters. The trading of dress patches is a common thread in the young women’s letters, if you’ll excuse the pun. As with her other letter, Matilda crowds her last thoughts into margins instead of using another piece of paper.

14.
Atlanta, Georgia
John Huffman to Anne Huffman
November 1, 1864

Atlanta
Nov the 1st 1864

Mifs Ann;
Dear Sister;
I recd your vary welcome letter a few days, and was very glad to hear from you, especially to hear that you was blefsed with good health. It is a great blessing to have good health, but far [emphasis by JJH]greater to have a pure heart, and a happy soul. I would like to know how you are getting along in a religious point of view. Do you feel that sacred love burning upon the altar of your heart, which the world can neither give, nor take away? Do you keep your soul untarnished and pure? Do you feel that glory that is unexpressible and full of glory? If not, put your trust in God and pray to him fervently, day and night and he will restore you. There is virtue and power in fervent prayr [begin pg. 2] I find (to my great joy) [( ) by JJH] when I grow cold and indifferent, if I come to God, acknowledge my sins and pray fervently and earnestly ["for forgivenefs" written between lines] He always hears and answers my petitions; and causes my soul to rejoice. There are Three things essential to religion; viz: faith, hope, and love. I hope and pray that you may ever be kept faithful. I have no war news to write. There are no special movements going on ["here" written between lines] There is but one corps (20th) [( ) by JJH] in Atlanta; the balance of the army is back near the R.R. operating against Hood. It is believed that we (the 20" Corps) [( ) by JJH] will leave here in a few days, and go on a raid; but this is vary uncertain. The report that Shermans army is in a critical situation, is untrue. We have always had enough to eat, and plenty to do. to keep us out of mischief.

There is no danger of starvation here. Forage was a little Scarce but we went out into the country, and got plenty. We will not be permitted to come home this fall to vote.

Please write immediately,
Your affectionate brother

J.J. Huffman

The letter is consistent with John's other letters in penmanship, spelling, and grammar.

We read a dramatic return of John's emphasis on religious faith and how vital it is for him. He is adamant in his concern for the depth of Anne's faith, hoping it is as deep as his. Why the abrupt return of such religious fervor? There is surely wide range for speculation. We have none of Anne's letters so cannot be helped directly by her correspondence. We may guess that there is something she has written or that someone else has written to John about her that elicits his earnest concern. This isn't the first letter in which John has written Anne about the importance of virtue, particularly hers. John could simply be feeling he's neglected his brotherly duty to his younger sister's welfare, in which case the statements are as much for his sake as for his sister's. Perhaps John is dissatisfied with Anne's failure to profess a religious faith equal to his. And, just maybe he is worried from afar that she may be susceptible to another affair.

The words he chooses for his closing line "Please write immediately" is telling. It seems more a command than a request. It isn't tempered as was his earlier request for the same response at the end of the letter he wrote from the Danville hospital. Another possibility is that we have a foreshadowing of what Sherman's army begins exactly two weeks after this letter is written. John may well know that Sherman has committed them all to leaving Atlanta in the hands of occupation forces, then heading into the "dark heart" of the Confederacy with his combat corps having no supply line nor any hope of reinforcements. It was a risky test of Sherman's belief that the Confederacy was a hollow shell with no organized defense within its core. Contemplating this would keep a lot of Union soldiers looking to their religious faith and families. We can easily believe John's fears that this may be the last letter Anne will get from him.

The admitted lack of news about the war or army life is interesting nonetheless. Again, we have a reference to "foraging" which the South called "pillaging". John acknowledges that the soldiers will not be coming home to vote in the fall.

This is the first letter with no return address. It may confirm that John knows it is unlikely any mail will be getting through for awhile. This could be the result of an order given to the men. In actual fact, once Sherman's army launched itself into the Savannah Campaign, or The March to the Sea as it is more (in)famously known, no one in the North knew its location nor its fate - be it triumph or annihilation. Only near the end of December, when Sherman sent his famous telegram to Lincoln presenting him with the city of Savannah as a Christmas present, was its success established.

15.
New Cumberland, Ohio
C.J. Huffman to Anne Huffman
November 3, 1864

New Cumberland Ohio
Nov. the 3rd /64

Dear Sister
Miss Ann,
Your most welcome letter came to hand this most (crossed out) morning and recd. my careful perusal and we was very glad to hear that you was well but I am sorry to tell you of the sad scene that has occurred here Peter Hoopingarner Died on last sunday and was buried on monday he died with the typhoid fever Elizabeth and marion laying to bed with it a good while but then they got better Peter took it and he was sick (pg. 2) Just three weeks and Rebecca Jane had it to but she has got better and now Barbara Ann is laying with it but she has just took it and we don't know how bad she will get and the old man is very poorly yet and the old woman has it very hard time of it for Lizzy and her is not able to do much yet and they can not get any girl for a great many people is afraid to go and Ann Eliza Suiter is laying very bad with it and the last we heard from her she was still getting worse the doctor has not much hopes of her recovery and Mary Wingate had it very bad to but she is getting better. (pg. 3) it is very sickly here Aunt Polly Huffman has been sick about it month and Mary Ann Mansfield is sick also but it is their old complaints that ails them you said you wanted to know if we had heard from the boys lately Georges got a letter from John last Friday and he had not been very well for several days but he was better when he rote he said David was well we have not heard from W. Bowman since he was taken prisoner Wesley Hoopingarner has deserted the Army Mary talks of coming in this fall but her folks thin she better not

until they all get well for it is (pg. 4) very sickly here and the fever is catching and she might take it we are all well except Matilda has the ague they was working at William Welshes below Sandyville close to the water and she took it while she was there I must close my letter and I want you to show it to Mike Kimmels for Hoopingarner has not wrote to them about Peter being dead so write at receipt your sister

C.J. Huffman

This is another of Jerry's home front letters. His comments: "faint blue lines on 9X7" paper folded vertically giving a four 41/2 wide by 7" high pages. Crescent over 3 stars embossed in upper left former of both first and third pages. Very newsy, about town and typhoid epidemic, and about war, Wes Hoop's desertion from the Army (joined the Confederates as you see later) and Wm Bowman's being prisoner. Both John and David were OK."

I have not seen the original of this letter, but I can tell from the copy that it is remarkably well-preserved. As with the others that were in this condition, this is likely due to the fact that they were handled very few times. For that reason and the fact that C.J has admirable penmanship, it is very easy to read except for some darkening where it was probably exposed to light or air for a while.

This is a truly dismal, despairing letter. Later in the letter collection, we learn of David's lingering death after being wounded, and we are rightfully shocked and saddened. Yet these deaths of men and women, youthful and elderly alike, are no less shocking and depressing for those who survive. We know C.J. is young so we can imagine how stricken and fearful she must be as she sees neighbors and childhood friends struck down. She must wonder if the pestilence will come to the Huffmans' home. Matilda is already ill, but at least not with "the typhoid". Peter Hoopingarner is 26. Rebecca Jane and Barbara Ann are two of his sisters. In her letter of September 28, Matilda writes that Pete Hoopingarner's baby died but that Pete was well. Now he is gone too.

It's interesting that C.J. refers to everyone by name except for the "old man" and "old lady". Presumably these are Peter's mother and father, George (63) and Christiana (58).

"C.J.'s" actual first name is Christina. She is Anne, Matilda, George, David, and John's younger sister. There are several scratch-outs where C.J. made corrections. Not only is her handwriting neat and legible, but she does a much better job of spelling than her sister-in-law Matilda. You can speculate on the reasons for this: a better education, more pride, even better "fine motor skills", as we would say today. However, C.J. was unmarried at the time and did not have a family to care for as Matilda did. There is no reference in this letter of sickness and death that C.J. wishes she were dead as Matilda had commented in her earlier one.

Most of the sickness is from typhoid fever. Often deadly then, it is rare today, for it is both preventable and treatable. My mother had typhoid fever when she was a child. She was quarantined and had a nurse; her diet was so restricted that she ate a rose in a vase by her bedside. When her mother discovered this, she started feeding Mom more regularly despite the doctor's orders. Ironically, typhoid is not "catching", but is contracted by consuming contaminated water or food.

C.J. writes that Matilda has the "ague". ".. they was working... below Sandyville close to the water and she took it while she was there". Ague is a malaria-like illness with aches, fever, and chills. It makes sense that she could have contracted it from a low-lying area possibly near the Ohio River. Who is the "they"? Is this Matilda, George's wife, or is it C.J.'s 23-year-old sister, also named Matilda?

C.J. mentions "W. Bowman". Of all the references to him, this is the most slight. She doesn't refer to him as Bill or Billy, or at the very least William. Maybe she does not know him as well, or this is just her own way of abbreviating his first name.

She writes Anne about the news of Wes Hoopingarner deserting the (Union) Army, but barely. Is it old news, a common occurrence, or that it just isn't that important to C.J. in her present state of mind? She doesn't seem to be nearly as upset by this as others. Understandably, William Bowman condemns him in a later letter. Jerry may be wrong about Wes Hoop's joining the Confederate Army. After taking the oath of allegiance to the Confederacy, the turncoats were simply released from prison with appropriate papers to avoid re-capture. What they did after that was up to them. Surely, it would be a long time, if ever, before they could go back to friends and family. Their desertion would be considered treason, cowardice, and betrayal.

Another mystery is - who is Mike Kimmels? It certainly seems that C.J. is sure Anne knows him. He is mentioned in none of the other letters, and I can find no information on him either in Indiana or Ohio during that period.

16.
New Cumberland, Ohio
Matilda Huffman to Anne Huffman
March 6, 1865

New Cumberland O
March the 6th 65

Miss E A Huffman
pretty Sister
How glad I am that I have the strength to write to you in answer to your kind letter which I rect too weeks ago and was very glad to hear from you but was sorrow to hear that you was crippled in your sholder but I hope that you are well again well Anne I have some gloryous knews to tell we have one of the prettyist babes that ever was born it was two weeks old yesterday (pg 2) it weighed Seven pounds when it was born ain't it a jolly wormer Kate was here and took care of us agin George is a making sugar this year he is in the camp and our little girls are a washing and I am a rocking the cradle and writing as the cradle rested six years it goes very well I want you to get a very nice name and send it to me for our babe you wanted me to ask mother wether you had the mumps and I have not seen mother yet but Kate says she thinks you had (pg 3) you wanted to know if we heard from Bowman lately we heard from him in Nov last and not since I do hope that he will be exchanged tell me if you ever hear of Wes Hoop we got a letter from our dear brother last week they was well there is a great deal of sickness hear at this time poor Anne Suiter had to leave this wourld I hope for a better one She died last monday She took sick in nov Her little Becky is very low the rest of the family is all better (pg 4) there is a great excitement hear the boys are nearly all volinteering I will give you some of their names George Strawn Isaac Dilly Isaac Sparks John Miser Sam Wingate James Dilly Uncle George Barricks George Leuther Tressel

they are all gone God only knows who will go next George has paid twenty five dollars this time to clear our t p he has paid eighty in all old aunt Polly Huffman is very low Catherine Albaugh is very bad with the fever now tell us when you are coming home. Write soon good by your sister
Matilda Huffman
Hoops are all well Barb was hear yesterday she brought me some sweet cakes
(Written upside down in upper margin of page four)
we are all well babe and all I wish you were hear to get some taffy
(Written upside down across the tops of pages 2 and 3.)

This is another of Jerry's letters. He observes: "Very newsy and lists soldiers drafted although just a month before end of war. The Barricks listed above are family members of my great, great grandmother. She married Sherrod who started Sherrodsville, Ohio, and produced Lizzie Sherrod. Lizzie married Patrick Daugherty, Aunt Beckie's father. The names Barrick and Sherrod both appear as street names in Sherrodsville now."

The Patrick Dougherty referred to in Jerry's notes is my own great-grandfather. Sherrodsville is a hamlet in east central Ohio.

Here is yet another form of addressing Anne. This time it is "Miss E Ann Huffman".

Again, I am judging only by seeing the copy, but this is another very well preserved letter. The only difficulty is the marks caused by the folds in the paper. Matilda's penmanship and spelling are both better in this one, so perhaps she is more relaxed despite the recent birth of another baby. However, unlike C.J., she cannot resist her desire to squeeze in the last bits of news in the margins.

The new arrival is, perhaps, the newsiest part of this letter. First, there is no mention of her pregnancy in her letter of September 28, 1864, though she would assumedly have been three months along. Why is she asking Ann to suggest a name for the new-born? Does Matilda really intend to wait for this letter to reach Anne, and for her to reply, before naming the baby? God forbid, but what if the baby died without a name? Additionally, there is no mention of the baby's gender - Boy? Girl? How is Anne to know? Perhaps this is just a courtesy, or maybe an inside joke. Or, even a reminder to Anne that she's not around to ask in person. We can yet again guess about Matilda's reference that the cradle has been empty for six years as to how welcome this baby is. At least it seems her girls are old enough to help with the chores. (Later the baby will be named Ruth.)

Matilda's husband is off at "camp". George could well be at sugar camp where maple trees would be tapped to make maple syrup, sugar, and candy for home use and barter. It's just about the right time of the year for it.

Why does she want to know whether or not Anne has had mumps? Today we may want to know if we had chicken pox so we can get an anti-shingles inoculation. But, back then...? I think that the Kate mentioned here is probably Catherine Huffman, another sister.

Anne has asked in a letter about the fate of Bill Bowman. She has received some letters from him, but evidently none since he was captured which is understandable.

Again the name of Wes Hoop (Hoopingarner) comes up, but in such a vague reference one wonders if Matilda thinks Anne might not know of his desertion.

George has paid another twenty-five dollars to avoid the draft. Many others who have avoided the draft so far have seemingly (to be uncharitable) seen the course of the war and decided to take the bonus. They enlisted hoping that the war would be over by the time they got to the front, or even close to it. Anne Suiter, who C.J. reported as being very ill in her letter of early November, has indeed died

Aunt Polly is still very ill.

17.
New Cumberland, Ohio
C.J. Huffman to Anne Huffman
March 9, 1865

New Cumberland O
March the 9th 1865

Mifs Ann Huffman

Dear Sister
This evening finds me seated for the purpose of answering your letter which came to hand some time ago and we were very glad to hear that you was well but there is a great deal of sicknefs here this winter. John Snitors family have had it hard through with the Typhoid fever and Mrs Snitor and two of the children died with it and Catharine and Raebecca are [probably "aren't"] died yet but they are getting better they have had the fever in the family about five months [begin pg. 2] and they have all had it except Dan and George and Catharine Albaugh had the fever too but she is now getting better. I suppose you have heard the news over at Georges they have a great big young daughter it weighed eleven pounds at first – I do no know what it would [weigh] <written below the line> now something lefs than a hundred I expect that it is pretty near three weeks old there is a great many boys enlisting I will give you the names of those that I know James Mills Samuel Wingate Isac Sparks William Sparks Isac Dilly Thomas McCaskey Columbus Cooper George Strawn and William Luther Tressel. They have enlisted for one year and they get five hundred dollars township bounty one hundred government bounty and twenty dollars a month while in service [begin pg. 3] George Strawn was here last Wednesday and he said they were going to start next monday Aunt Polly Huffman is laying sick yet and I do not think she will ever get any better for she is very weak she has to spit in cloths nearly all the time and they have been

sitting up with her nearly all winter and some of us has go down every few nights I believe I have nothing more to write this time.

No more at present

your sister
Write soon

C.J. Huffman

P.S. Said[?] says you must hurry and get married and fetch your man in here and let us see him If you can't read this send it back and I will read [?] it for you fo I wrote it with a short stick.

This is another 'home front' letter. As did her sister-in-law, Matilda, C.J. spells Anne's first name without an "e". David addresses her as "E.A.", John as "Anne". The brothers are probably just more formal in writing style, and the young women less so.

As with Matilda's letter, this letter is full of the news that young women like to know. There is no preaching about the value of a life of virtue or questioning about Anne's religious life. C.J.'s letter has less about domestic life than Matilda's for, after all, she is unmarried and only 19 or 20 when she writes.

It's interesting to try to read between the lines in this letter. C.J. twice remarks on the large size of the new baby "over at Georges". She has either a sense of humor or is perhaps being "catty" when she writes "I do not know what it would weigh now something less than a hundred I expect". I prefer to think the former. The new baby is, of course, the same one mentioned in Matilda's letter dated just three days earlier. C.J., though she doesn't say it in so many words, seems to be pretty "grossed out" by Aunt Polly Huffman and not pleased about having to "...go down every few nights". Equally, her accounting of the cumulative bounty and pay of the new volunteers can be taken two ways. She may be admiring how much the new recruits are granted or she may be comparing their "patriotism" with that of her brothers and other local boys who enlisted almost two years earlier for no bounty. It's possible these new soldiers have just reached the minimum age for enlistments, or they may indeed have looked at the progress of the war and made a cold calculation about the money versus the well-known hardships and risks.

The great amount of sickness in the one family, and the community in general, makes it clear that illness wasn't just a threat to soldiers. I wonder how many other families had similar sicknesses that winter. And, I wonder if it makes Anne glad she wasn't in New Cumberland the winter of 1863-64. We have none of her letters, so we don't know if she is homesick or not.

There is a cross-reference in this letter. In it, C.J. relates that one of the new recruits is George Strawn. In his second Parkersburg letter, William Bowman writes to David, "...tell George Strawn to write to me for I would like to here from him and his family." About half the recruits C.J. names are also mentioned in Matilda's recent letter. It seems the Tressel boys both have the same middle name. For what it's worth, you may have noticed by now that there seems to be a general lack of variety of given names in New Cumberland. The Strawns and Tressels are close neighbors of the Huffmans, and the Tressels are kin.

A mystery lies within this letter. Who is the man that C.J. refers to when she writes that Ann(e) "...should hurry and get married and fetch your man in here and let us see him."? It certainly isn't William (whom she marries after the war), for he is serving in the East and has only recently been exchanged as a prisoner-of war. William is also unlikely for another reason. He is a childhood friend of all the Huffmans. Matilda writes of his capture ("poor Bill") in her letter to Anne, and he has lived with their uncle, so there is no need to "... fetch (him) in here and let us see him" for they have likely seen him many times. Is it possible Anne did have a beau in Indiana previous to William? C.J. is young so she may be doing some girlish romantic misinterpretation in what her older, perhaps bolder, sister has written.

As before, C.J. writes pretty well. She spells accurately and has a fair grasp of grammar. Her great weakness is in the use of end mark punctuation and upper case letters. While this occurs in other letters to a degree, it is pronounced here. C.J. may just be in a rush, excited to write. It does make it harder for the modern reader. Even after a dozen or more readings, I found myself pausing to find where one thought stops and another starts. I wonder how Anne did with it. C.J.'s penmanship is also only fair this time.

This is very similar to the paper the brothers used in their letters: blue-lined, folded to make four surfaces, and with a maker's mark embossed in the upper left corner of the first page. In this case the mark is no longer legible.

The last sentence of the "P.S." is written around the corner of the paper even though the fourth page is not used. I can only guess at what the words "...send it back and I will read (ed. emphasis) it for you" mean. Does she mean she will rewrite the letter? I suppose the expression "...I wrote it with a short stick" was well understood at the time. I can only guess that it meant that her pen was not of the best quality. If this was written in pencil, it would mean more, but it is written in ink which has faded badly. Perhaps she is apologizing for using a pen with a worn nib.

18.
Goldsboro, North Carolina
John Huffman to Anne Huffman
March 28, 1865

Goldsboro, N.C.

March 28 /65

My Dear Sister:
I know it will be sad news to hear of the Death of our Dear Brother David! He was mortally wounded in a charge on the rebel works, on the 16" inst. after intense suffering of nearly ten days he departed this life on the 25" about midnight. This will be painful news to you; but I can recomend Christ as a Comforter, go to Him, and he will sustain you. I am sorely afflicted. I feel as though I had lost the dearest, and only friend I had, here in the army, but Christ is my comforter; when I come to him He Sustains me [begin pg. 2] I ask the assistance of your prayrs I feel need of them, you have mine daily. Not being certain that you are in Ind. yet, I will write nomore this time. I would ask you to live so that you may [meet] <written between lines> our Dear Brother in Heaven. He gave evidence before he died, that he was going to Christ. please write soon, and give me a word of consolation.

Your aggrieved brother,

Ambulance Corps
2" Brig. 3 Div 20" A.C.
Goldsboro, N.C.

It's a strange thing. You'd think I'd be detached from feelings for something which happened more than 150 years ago to someone who was not even an ancestor. You'd think it would be an exercise something akin to reading a history book, especially since I'd read all this before. Instead, I found it difficult to approach a re-edit of this

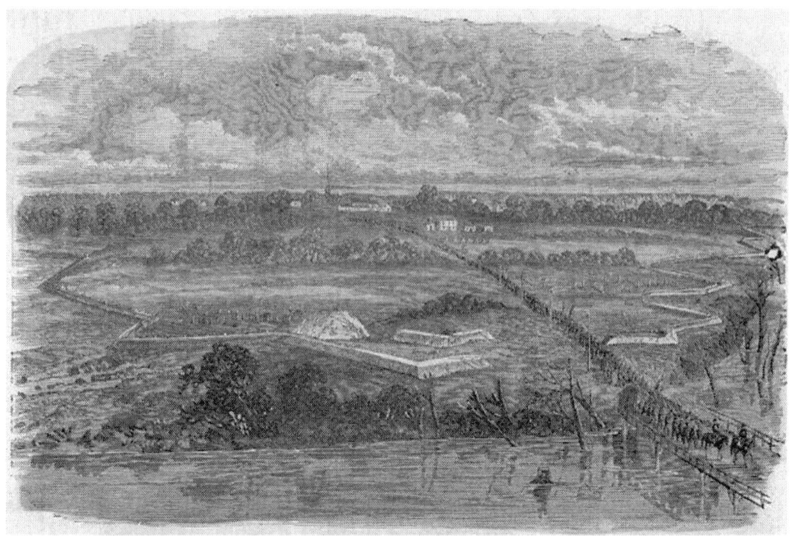

General Schofield's army on its march to Goldsboro, NC

letter. Indeed, I put it off for a good while. Where on previous letters I looked forward to the work, this one I approached with discernible dread. It was a "goosebump" moment, to be sure, but a little different than the one I had when I learned that William was at Andersonville. It took months before I learned that fact through the leisurely, logical process of research. Most of the impact of this letter came that first night in the Daugherty's basement rec-room. Over the years, between my initial work on the collection and this effort, I'd not forgotten the shock of that first reading. Of course, I knew what had happened. Through the process of re-reading and re-writing the letters, plus re-thinking and even re-researching each one, I had become attached to the Huffman family and to William Bowman. In my fascination with how the farm boy and the young school teachers had suffered in adjusting to a life so different, difficult, unexpected, and fearful, as a result of their spontaneously answering of their country's call, I'd come to know them. I considered them almost to be friends, and even went so far as to put myself in their place. In short, I'd come to truly care for them.

Notice the date of David receiving a mortal wound (March 15) and his death (March 25). The battle in which he died occurred less than a month before Lee surrendered to Grant at the Appomattox Court House; less than six weeks before Joe Johnston surrendered his Carolina forces to Sherman. Few soldiers want to die in battle, of course, especially when the outcome is no longer in doubt, the issue settled. To die when your death makes no difference is especially grievous. The fact that the fight in which David was mortally wounded was enabled, if not necessitated, by a Northern newspaper's printing of Sherman's order of march, makes it especially egregious. Horace Greeley's *New York Tribune* published information which allowed Joe Johnston to maneuver his army into a position making another major battle unavoidable. David and several hundred others died as a result. Sherman did not forget, nor forgive. Not long after the end of the war, he refused to talk to Greeley upon being introduced, famously snubbing him.

I received records from the Bureau of Archives that show David "Died March 27th 1865 at Goldsboro, N.C. from effects of wounds received in battle March 16, 1865 at Averysboro (actually Averasborough) N.C". The record further shows that the "...wound (was) to the right breast". I found three different dates for David's death: March 25, 26 and 27. John was personally affected by this death, so I tend to honor his notation of the 25th. Other record keepers were certainly very busy writing and copying such information, and thus errors were not unlikely.

John writes that David was "...mortally wounded in a charge on the rebel works". If David was still indeed in the Ambulance Corps, why does this occur? The record shows that he was still attached to the A.C. at the time of his death. Certainly, it is possible that he was attending the wounded on the battlefield when he was shot. One would hope that the ball which killed him was a random shot.

We can only imagine what David (and John) went through in those "...ten days of intense suffering." At least David had John with him through his suffering. It is easy to speculate that he would have survived with better medical care.

John writes "our Dear Brother in Heaven. He gave evidence before he died, that he was going to Christ."

Again, I do not want to parse these letters too closely, but I can't help wondering if this "evidence" is a special relief to John. Was David's prior depth of faith a concern to him? We'll never know, of course, but in his single surviving letter, David not once makes reference or reverence to a religious outlook for himself, much less urging one on Anne. He mainly expresses the ancient, classic concerns of the foot soldier: the food, the weather, the march, the fighting.

19.
New Cumberland, Ohio
William Bowman to Anne Huffman
April 27, 1865

April 27, 1865
New Cumberland Tuscarawas Co.
Ohio
Miss Ann Huffman
Dear Friend it is with pleasure that I seat my sealf this morning to let you know that I am well and I hope when these few lines come to hand they will find you enjoying the same great blessing of health I received your kind letter yesterday and I was glad to hear from you once more and to hear that you are enjoying good health I was sorry to hear that David was dead I thought we would get home to gether and we would have some good times to gether but I hope John and the rest of the boys will get home. The prospect of the war being over and I hope it will the knabours is all well as far as I know your aunt mary is not getting anny better I do not think she will get well at tall [begin pg. 2]
Ruth J Davy told me to write to you that she is well and hearty and as big a mischief as ever ann I have a verry lonsome time since I come home but I have good times I had (s)hard times all last summer I think I will have better times this summer the boys is all gone from her but a few I will tell you a little about Wes Hoopingarner he deserted and joined the rebbel army I never thought he had that little principle a bout him as that comes to he never need come back in this country when I was in prision I said that I would die befour I would gow and take the oath of a leigence I thought it was more honor to die and honerable death than to gow ot and disgrace my sealf I have got only four mounths to serve anny more but I do not think there will be anny more fighting
[begin pg. 3] You must come home when John and the boys comes home I have not got verry mutch to

write at the preasnt time I will write more the next time you must excuse all bad writing and spelling sow <here there is an illegible word, but not "I"> will close for the preasant write as soon as this come to hand from your friend W. Bowman

Mis Ann Huffman
good by

This letter was written by William while he was home on leave after being processed through the system for soldiers released from Confederate prisons. He writes that he still has four months left on his enlistment service. This is borne out by the date of his discharge.

The letter is quite poignant in the places where William sorrows over David not being there for the better times after the war, and when he tells Ann(e) how lonesome he is with nearly all the "boys gone from here but a few." Once again he sounds more like a farm boy than a cynical seasoned veteran. We know from C.J. Huffman's March 1865 letter the names of nine local boys who'd enlisted at the time of high bounties. William must have only missed them by a month. I wonder how they would feel about their choice after seeing how William must have looked after six or seven months at Andersonville and hearing his stories. You get the feeling that his homecoming was not the joyous experience he had anticipated.

William writes "I had hard times all last summer." That has to be one of the wildest understatements of the Libby and Andersonville experiences which any inmate could make. It's surely because he did not want to frighten Ann(e) too much, but still, reducing the hell of Andersonville to "hard times"! Perhaps he thinks this understatement will help. Almost certainly, there is that reluctance gripping William here that nearly all combat veterans share, no matter the war. How do you speak of unspeakable experiences? Where does he begin? How can mere words (of which he possesses so few for writing) make anyone besides another who was there understand? And, if they were there, no words are necessary.

He shows stronger feelings when he writes about Wes Hoopingarner deserting and joining the rebels. Here he sounds more like an angry veteran, as he has every right to. His spelling becomes noticeably worse, for instance. His strong statement of his own principle is far more than the easy sort of hyperbole young men can profess when war still seems an exciting adventure. William's courage and honor have been tested, not only by battle, but by a true and terrible ordeal beyond combat. When he says "I thought it more honor to die and honerable death than to go out and disgrace myself", he is not exaggerating. He did very nearly die. If he, like Wes Hoopingarner, had agreed to desert, to take the oath of allegiance to the Confederacy, he would have been released from Andersonville. He refused, though the temptation must have been strong.

William writes to Ann(e) "You must come home when John and the boys comes home." This seems to be evidence that the Huffmans' home was in New Cumberland. We do know that George and Matilda's family was still in New Cumberland. It could be that William thinks they should just be coming back for a visit. This isn't likely. What's more likely is that William really does especially want Ann back just because he likes her.

The penmanship is this letter is noticeably neater than in either of his earlier letters to David, though his spelling is no better. Again, he apologizes for it. And, even though it is pretty good, he also apologizes for his writing. There are no commas, only one end mark, and few capital letters beginning sentences. None of that "ss" written as "fs" stylishness occurs either.

I wondered about the improvement in the neatness of the handwriting. At first, I chalked it up to the advantages of his being at home - having plenty of time to write, few friends to spend time with, a better place to write, no hassles or distractions of army life, and no fear about further fighting. That made sense. Later, I put two and two together and came up with a plausible reason why William wanted this letter to be his best work. He was writing to his future wife. So, he very well might have fancied Anne even then.

20.
Raleigh, North Carolina
John Huffman to Anne Huffman
April 29, 1865

Raleigh, N.C.
April 29" /65

Dear Sister,
Your kind and affectionate letter of the 16' inst. came to hand yesterday, but I cannot answer all your questions at present, I have not time, I expect to come home and tell them to you; which will be much more pleasant than writing. Johnston has surrendered his entire army to Gen Sherman and the war is virtually over - hostilities have ceased and we expect to start for Washington City next monday. I expect to be in Indiana about the first of June, [begin pg. 2] and perhaps I will come by and See you and if you want to come home with me, you can do So. I have not time to write more at present. I will expect a reply by the time I reach Washington. Do not delay writing.

Your affectionate brother
J.J. Huffman
Co. I 85th Ind. Vol.
2" Brig. 3"Div. 20 A.C.
Mifs E. A. Huffman

This is a brief letter - the shortest of any save that written by William from Andersonville.

In writing back to Anne, John alludes to"...all your questions", but in the same sentence replies "...I cannot answer .... I have not time". We do not know what Anne's questions are, but they may be more than John wants to consider at this time. Or, he may feel that he doesn't have the words to answer. Even with the fighting over, there is a very real prospect that John actually doesn't have time to write a carefully considered reply. As at the end of World War II, there was a hue and cry to bring the boys back home as soon as possible. John already speaks of leaving

Johnston and Sherman meet on Hillsboro road

for Washington, D.C. in less than a week and being back in Indiana by the beginning of June, only a month away. Besides his military duties, frequent movements would be necessary.

John's records show that the 85th Indiana Volunteers participated in the Grand Review, the triumphal day-long marching past of Union soldiers in Washington, D.C. on May 26th and 27th, 1865. The review involved so many units that it stretched into two days.

John seems to be ambivalent about whether he'll stop by and see his sister when he returns to Indiana: "Perhaps (author's emphasis) I will come by and see you." Is this more evidence of a rift between John and Anne? His statement "... if you want to come home with me, you can do So." shows an equal diffidence. Perhaps this is a subtle recognition of Anne's independent nature as has been latent in more than one letter. By contrast, John is decisive in his closing sentences. "I will expect a reply by the time I reach Washington. Do not delay writing."

Evidently, John still considers New Cumberland home, even though he doesn't stay there, if indeed he returns at all just after the war. The 1870 census shows him living in Indiana with a young wife and family. He does not return to teaching for his occupation is listed as "merchant".

21.
New Cumberland, Ohio
Matilda Huffman to Anne Huffman
May 18, 1865

New Cumberland O

May the 18th 65
Miss E A Huffman
Kind sister
I rect your letter too weeks ago and I will try and write I would had wrote sooner but was waiting for a letter from brother John we rec't a letter from him yesterday he is well and he is coming home well sister glory to God the war is over but sorry to say we have lost a dear brother indeed but Gods will be done we had to give up our good old president but wo unto the rebbels now (pg 2)
poor old uncle George Hoopingarner died last sunday about three oclock PM and was buried monday they met at the house at one O and the surmond was preached at the house by McCale it was a large bruian old aunty is well and the rest of the family old Aunt Polly Huffman is very poorly mothers are all well George works at his trade he gets one dollar and seventy 1.75 per day and Mary and Maggy goes to school and I and pet are left alone I am making pet a knew dress she has three too make I got her one (pg 3)
and the others was give to her We call her Ruth Christeene she is three mounths old tomorrow and weight 20 pounds lully for the babe I must close and write John a letter write and tell us when you are coming home do write soon good by believe yours till Huffman
PS Nick Hoop wrote home that Wes was taken prisonor and then enlisted in the rebble army and is poroled and will be home soon
Matilda Huffman (pg 4)
George Huffman
Matilda Huffman

Mary Huffman
Maggie Huffman
Ruth Huffman
chew some of my cloves
tell us when your a
coming home

This is the last of the home front letters from Jerry. His notes are: "four-folded 8 x10, faint blue lines, floral embossed mark in upper left corner of first and third pages. Interesting fact that Wesley enlisted in the Rebel Army, was later paroled and is coming home this date being after the end of the war. Can you imagine the problem he may have when he gets back after being a turncoat??? Note her sentiment: "We have to give up our good old president, but wo unto the rebels now".

This is another very nicely preserved letter. Even the copy is extremely clear to read. Matilda seems to be much more relaxed in writing this letter. Her handwriting seems less hurried, and her spelling is somewhat better. There is also a variation in the closing in that Matilda signs herself as "till" and then after the PS as Matilda. Perhaps she is more relaxed because the war is over, her husband is safe, and her other daughters are now old enough to go to school and help with chores.

The Hoopingarners are family, so the news that George has died is especially important. He is the second Hoopingarner to die at home. Surely, Matilda knew about Wes's desertion and treason before she started this letter, so it is speculation as to why she seemingly trivialized his treachery by adding it as a postscript. Was she trying to soften the news?

I agree with Jerry in wondering at the news that Wes Hoopingarner is planning on coming home. If this is true, what does he expect his reception will be?

There is only a brief reference to David's death. There are no thoughts as to how close he came to coming home safely. Grief was not expressed in writing, but borne privately.

JIM DOHREN

I agree with Jerry in his comment that the assassination of Lincoln caused people to expect vengeance on the South, as indeed was the case.

The new baby "Ruth Christeene" has a pet name, in fact it is "Pet". It seems as if Matilda is more comfortable with the new "babe" than she was in the last letter when she not only didn't refer to its gender, but evidently hadn't named it, called it a "little wormer", and referred to the fact that it was six years younger than her next youngest. In addition, she asks Anne a "lully" for Pet. I guess this is shorthand for a lullaby.

She takes the time and space to list the names of the family members at the end of the letter.

Aunt Polly is still ailing. Poor Aunt Polly! She has passed from being a cause for real concern to not much more than an afterthought in less than a year.

22.
Indianapolis, Indiana
John Huffman to Anne Huffman
June 28, 1865

Indianapolis, Ind
June 28 /65

Dear Sister
I am now in Indianapolis, Ind and I expect to be paid off <"today" written between the lines> and receive my final discharge. I will then return to Clay Co. Ind. where I expect to remain for two or three weeks, and then I think I will go to Ohio, and if you wish to go with me I will be very happy to stop in Henry Co. and have you go home with me. I expect to be ready to Start in a little more than three weeks. [begin pg.2] You will please write immediately on the receipt of this and let me know what you will do. My health is good and I hope you enjoy the same blefsing.

Yours affectionately
J.J. Huffman

direct to Bowling Green
Clay Co. Ind

This is the last letter in the collection. It seems to be just a brief note sent out to give Anne some time to prepare for John's arrival to visit her.

The letter is true to John's writing in every way. This one, though brief, is the very best for consistency with modern spelling and usage. In fact, it's surprising to me how little change there has been in almost 150 years.

The letter does confirm, if we needed it, that the Huffmans' home is in Ohio.

As in previous letters, John shows doubt, if not bewilderment, about what Anne wants to do and even where she is living. This has been apparent before. Why is this? Does she not answer his questions? Are her answers vague? Does she keep changing her mind? Is she resistant to his questioning and resentful of his instructions? Does he simply ignore her answers which are unsatisfactory to him? Perhaps she has thoughts of returning to Ohio now that the war is over. John's apparent confusion is similar to what we read in his letters to Anne back in 1863. I speculated before that Anne seems to have been an independent minded young woman. If John's attitude is typical of the rest of the Huffman men, then it is little wonder that she has moved to Indiana.

Despite using the word "please" John continues the seemingly presumptive tone toward Anne at the end of yet another of his letters "You will please write immediately... and let me know where you are." It's interesting that he doesn't even know that.

The *pro forma* concern for good health appears almost as an afterthought.

One thing that hasn't been mentioned is that both brothers never close their letters to Anne with a familiar name like "John" or "David", only initials. This is probably a matter of form rather than emotion.

At first I was puzzled by the postscript "direct to Bowling Green, Clay Co. Ind". Then, I put that together with John's information that he would be traveling to Clay County after his discharge and staying there for two or three weeks. This is his return address for Anne's (hopefully) quick response.

This paper is even more fascinating than the "Cock-a-doodle Doo. On to Victory" paper which John used in his letter from the hospital in Danville, Kentucky. It is a bit smaller than that used in other letters. What truly distinguishes it are the embellishments. Printed at the top of the first page is a large letterhead stating "THIS SHEET OF PAPER AND ENVELOPE IS FURNISHED BY THE INDIANA SANITARY COMMISSION Being purchased with Funds contributed by the SOLDIER'S FRIENDS BACK HOME". All the above is printed in varied styles.

There is an accompanying poem:

Fly little missive to my cherished home,
And cheer the loving hearts to me so dear,
I'll follow in honor when I can come,

And leave 'Our Flag' in TRIUMPH floating here!

Taken out of context, a bit of doggerel, I suppose. Nevertheless, it was purchased and provided with gratitude by the citizens and appreciated and used by the soldiers. In place of a water mark, there is an engraving of a distinguished bearded gentleman surrounded by the words:

Indiana Soldiers
The Pride of the State
And the Glory of the Army

This is one of the few letters with a surviving envelope. It has an engraving identical to that described above in the upper left front corner where we would write a return address. The envelope is addressed to "Mifs Ann Huffman Middleton".

John has made a large flourish at the bottom of the paper to help clear the pen nib of ink.

AFTERWORD

Over the many years I've had these letters and the dozens of times I've read them, I've come to firmly believe that all letters written from fields of battle back home, and the process in reverse, are far more than merely communication. What they tell us is of what most of us have never nor would realistically ever wish to experience. They tell of sacrifice, hardship, loyalty, devotion, glory, honor, adventure, good and evil. To me, though, they speak most of trust.

William, John and David had trust that the war was just, that what they were doing was right. At the beginning of the war, there was a belief that the fighting would be brief, that it would all be a great adventure taking them far from their plain rural lives as farmer and school teacher. They probably took for granted that their government would match their sacrifice and loyalty by taking care of them, providing them with adequate arms and supplies, medical care, and competent leadership. They knew they'd be with their friends and didn't consider how much they'd miss home.

That early in the war, they well may have felt the importance of honor and duty in their sacrifice with faith in God, the Constitution, the law of the land, and their government. They must have felt that what they were sacrificing would in some ways make a better future for their country and its people no matter their status, free or slave.

Surely, there were visions of coming home safe – victorious and acclaimed as conquering heroes. God was on their side. He would protect them and provide them with a bountiful life as a result of their good service and their faithfulness to Him.

In a somewhat careless way, they assumed that the homefolks would miss them badly, worry constantly about them, write faithfully, and hang on every word of their own letters. Equally they assumed that somehow the fields would be farmed and the children taught.

Not all the trust was on the part of the volunteers like our soldier letter writers. Those back home at least tried to maintain faith that somehow as the war dragged on, the terrible casualty lists lengthened, and dreaded letters arrived announcing wounds, sickness, capture and death, that their kinfolk would come back safe and sound, and a good life, maybe even a better life would commence.

We look back now from a distance of a century and a half wondering, reflecting with admiration, perhaps even envying in a way their devotion and naiveté. We can shake our heads at their gullibility, but we must never laugh nor call them foolish.

* * * * * * *

Readers may be wondering what happened to the seven letter writers after the war ended. Here is what I learned:

William Bowman never returned to active duty after his exchange. This is not surprising given the physical condition that he was in after Andersonville, and the short time between his return from prison and the end of the war. Military records show that he was mustered out on June 23, 1865, at Camp Chase, Ohio, along with other surviving members of his company. He was given an honorable discharge. Indeed, this must have been a bittersweet day for him and the rest of the 126th Ohio fortunate enough to be there.

His claim of friendship with Anne Huffman was evidently mutual for they married in 1868. William returned to his job as a farmer, and the couple eventually owned their own farm in eastern Ohio, resuming their lives near New Cumberland. Anne and William had three children. The first, born in 1869, did not live long. William does not provide the child's name on one of his pension applications. Perhaps it had been so long that he'd forgotten, but the baby's name was Nora. Two other children were born - Mary in 1870 and Jesse (pronounced "Jess") in 1873. Jesse married my mother's Aunt Becky Daugherty, and a good thing at that, for it is through the Daugherty family that I received the letters. They continued to reside in New Cumberland where I recall visiting them in the 1950s. Despite or maybe because of his crippling rheumatism, William becomes active in the

GAR (Grand Army of the Republic was a fraternal organization of Civil War veterans established in 1866) serving as Commander of the J.J. Alexander Post in Warsaw, Ohio, from at least 1896 to 1925 when he dies, the oldest and last of those involved in the correspondence.

Anne Huffman Bowman, the collector of the letters, and the initial protector of the trove, married William Bowman and had three children as stated above. The 1860 census records include her younger brother, Martin, in the household, as well as that subject of speculation, Leroy Huffman, who is listed as Leroy Dolvin. The 1870 census lists him as Dolvin L. Huffman, and the 1880 census lists him as Leroy Huffman. Anne and William had a long marriage. Anne was still living at the time of the 1920 census which shows her age as 78. At that time, they had been married 52 years. Anne died in the 1920 census year at the age of 79.

Anne's faithful, anxious, and rather stridently caring brother, John Huffman, returned to Indiana and stayed there, though he seems not to have taken up his old profession as a school master. This is certainly understandable considering his war experiences. In November of 1865, only a few months after returning from the war, he married Sarah Ellen Van Cleve who was only 18 compared to John's 34. Sarah and John had six children, the first born in 1866, and the last in 1885. John is first listed as a merchant in the 1870 census report. By 1890, he lists himself as a "capitalist". They are a two-income family as Sarah is shown to be a milliner. John lives into the new century, passing away in 1904 at the age of 72. He has an impressive granite tombstone at the Poland Chapel Cemetery in Poland, Indiana, so maybe he was a successful capitalist at that.

David, of course, does not survive the war. He is buried in North Carolina at the Raleigh National Cemetery, Plot 5. 311.

Joyful, loving Matilda and her husband George Huffman raised three girls to adulthood, though just barely in the case of their oldest daughter, Mary, who died in 1881 at the age of 22. Matilda's mother Mary passed away that same year. George died in 1879. Matilda survived him by 13 years, dying in 1892 at the age of 54.

Christina, also known as C.J., Anne's effervescent, romantic younger sister didn't marry until she was 32 years old, when she became Mrs. Harvey P. Shiltz. The couple had three odd-year born children: Minerve in 1885, Jennie in 1887, and Jerry in 1889.

Ruth J. Davy was the youngest of the letter writers and the only one who was not a Huffman family member, save William Bowman. Ruth married John Wheadon when she was 29 years old. The couple had three children - Edward, Mary, and Ralph. They continued to live near New Cumberland.